WITH
BENEDETTA BELLONI

101 WAYS
to look
SLIMMER AND TALLER

(BLACK AND WHITE EDITION)

How to lengthen your body
and get a taller-appearing figure
while visually cutting off extra pounds
through no-cost hints that will make you feel
thinner and more attractive, and help you
achieve a chic look and unique French allure.

ENGLISH EDITION
EDITED BY CREATESPACE

Acknowledgments

A big thank-you *from the bottom of my heart*
goes first of all to my little helper, Leandro,
who has participated with passion and patience (lots of it!)
in the making of all the photo shoots for the book.

I also would like to thank all my friends from near and far,
who are my only and unique source of inspiration.

ISBN: 1984978756
ISBN 13: 978-1984978752

Website:
www.ladonnadicharme.it

Table of Contents

DOWNLOAD YOUR
FREE *COPY OF THE E-BOOK!*
(only for purchases on Amazon.com)

Important Note
to the Black and White
Edition:

The original edition of this book is in full color. We decided to also publish an edition in black and white, to make the book available at a more affordable price. Although the majority of the photos contained in the book are also understandable in black and white, not all of them are. Therefore, for a better understanding of the content, we recommend downloading your free copy of the e-book on your tablet or PC (for those who buy the paperback on Amazon.COM, the e-book is free of charge) and view it with Kindle Cloud Reader (it's free and easy to use) in order to view the images in full color.

Furthermore, depending on the chosen device, the photos displayed may appear smaller than the originals; to fix this issue, it is sufficient to click or double-tap on each image to view it on full screen.

Preface

This book, as the title says, is a manual that contains 101 "tips and tricks" to look **slimmer and taller**, supported by pictures that show the most effective ways to **choose and combine garments in order to appear thinner in no time**, while **visually adding a few inches to the legs** and getting a visibly slimmer silhouette without any need to lose weight.

The aim to look thinner is indeed so deep-seated in women's thoughts that most of us are practically always dieting, regardless of whether the sensation of carrying around a few extra pounds is real or not.

Well, from now on, with the help of the suggestions of this book, **you can forget dieting!**[1]

You will discover indeed **how to "visually" lose several pounds** effortlessly, and in just a minute, simply applying some "optical tricks" that allow you to slim your silhouette.

You will learn how to choose the garments most suitable for you and how to match them, harmonizing your curves instead of covering them.

Moreover, to follow the hints illustrated in this manual, you won't need to buy new clothes, because **just a few simple changes in matching items that you already have will allow you to make the most of yourself.**

---

[1] *However, eating healthy food and taking some exercise is always a recommendation because it also helps you with feeling and looking younger.*

7

And if you want to do some shopping, in this manual you will also find some useful **guidelines to pick out garments that can enhance your physique while slimming your silhouette**, visually hiding a few extra pounds.

You will also learn how **sometimes it can be enough just changing one item, modifying a detail** (such as the hem), or playing around with accessories to get a result that flatters your body, giving you a taller-appearing figure.

You will see how choosing a different color or a different fabric can help you **look not only thinner but also more beautiful and self-confident**, and you will also discover that **it is not always necessary to wear incredibly high heels to look slimmer** (in fact, in some cases, the truth is quite the opposite).

You will learn how drawing attention to the cutest point of your body while at the same time **shaping your curves and highlighting them instead of hiding** them can assure a really lovely outcome, thanks to the fact that **the eye perceives the clothes much more than your actual figure**.

In short, you will find out how to look thinner and more attractive *today*, achieving a truly feminine, classy, and always chic look, while **boosting and enhancing your unique allure.**

Introduction

101 Ways to Look Slimmer and Taller is a look-book, as most of its 101 hints are accompanied by pictures of **outfits specifically selected** with the aim of **slimming the silhouette while lengthening the legs**.

Unlike most look-books, however, the recommended items and combinations are not just those of the latest trend—which is going to change in a few weeks—but **timeless ensembles, effective for any style, to obtain a thinner silhouette**.

In addition, **the photos do not portray a twenty-year-old, six-foot-tall, hundred-pound girl**—who looks good in anything—but rather yours truly, that is to say, **a short-statured woman, and furthermore, with even shorter legs.** A woman who, if she doesn't pay attention to what she's wearing, can easily wind up looking entirely formless (there are also some pics of Benedetta, who, despite being taller—five foot five—has been trying for years to get rid of thigh fat, while her hips always remain quite chubby, despite dieting and massage).

All the snapshots, as you will see, are entirely "homemade," and they have not been photoshopped or modified, which guarantees that all tips indeed really work.

The pictures you see side by side, which show **the DOs (pictures on the right) and the DON'Ts (pictures on the left)**, were generally taken just a few minutes apart. We did not use slimming lingerie, and neither did we eat an elephant between one photo and the other (the only extra trick I used was a padded bra, which always helps to make the waist look thinner).

The differences you will see are only due to **a few visual geometric tricks** that **can completely change the overall effect of the same outfit** by just shifting some detail on one single item.

You, too, can change from a Cinderella who feels short or with some extra pounds into **a taller-appearing, elegant, and chic woman**.

You will soon become more attractive and self-confident, thus creating a positive cycle, because when you feel more beautiful and self-confident, **you gain a poise that will *actually* make you look taller**.

Some tips, as you will see, remain much the same between summer and winter: the "geometric" rule does not change, but you need to **adjust it to the different seasons** as well as to the different types of garments.

As for the colors, we deliberately chose to **use mostly neutral colors to make the examples more understandable** also for the Kindle version, being the Kindle screen in black and white (though **we recommend downloading a copy of the e-book also on your PC or tablet, to see it in full color**). It will then be up to you to replace neutral and classical tonalities with other shades, depending on the colors that are most suitable for your skin tone or on your favorite pairings[2].

From a technical point of view, it should be pointed out that, as the suggestions are accompanied by photos of me or of Benedetta, you will likely find more inspiration in this book if you happen to have similar physical characteristics—that is to say, if you would like to look taller, with longer, leaner legs and narrower hips. However, we have also included some hints that can work equally well for different physical types **because if your main goal is**

---

[2] In my previous book, *How to Become a Woman of* Charme, you can find many tips to make the most of different color combinations.

looking thinner, any trick that makes you look taller will achieve the same result.

Besides, don't forget that every woman is different, and for this reason, **all the tips should always be verified on your own**, preferably with the help of a selfie (which can also help you to have a true awareness of your figure from behind).

Remember, moreover, that **you can also choose to wear something that is not the most flattering for your figure**: if you are aware of it, **you can easily minimize it in multiple ways**, for example, by adding an item that draws attention to itself and away from your imperfections.
Much depends on the occasion, but also—and above all— on how comfortable you feel with the people you are going to meet.

For example, if you are invited to a dinner party among dear old friends, you may want to wear a dress that you particularly like, even though you know that maybe it is not the most suitable to hide your hips. This is because when you are with the people whom you like the most, you feel self-confident, attractive, and appreciated no matter what you are wearing. If you feel beautiful and charming, this is reflected in the way you move and walk, and any imperfection remains unnoticed.

Yet, on other occasions, such as a dinner with your mother-in-law (who relentlessly makes unpleasant remarks on everything you are wearing), a lunch with your boss (who never misses an opportunity to criticize you), a date with the man of your dreams, and all the occasions **when you need some extra self-confidence,** this can be dealt with by using the suggestions that we will cover together!

Just by applying them, **you will instantly feel prettier, more attractive, and better-looking, and this will be reflected in your smile and in your approach to those around you**, allowing you to feel—and be—genuinely irresistible.

What is the proof that these tips work?

The fact that despite my short stature (five feet two inches), *all* my friends who are five foot five or so (which is the average height both for Italian and for US women) tell me, "You are not short! You're as tall as I am," and they do not realize that those 3 inches can indeed be an abyss.

Think about it: if you are five foot five, would you ever tell a friend of yours who is five foot eight, "I am as tall as you are"? No.

Yet, the difference is exactly the same.

This fact, however, only confirms one thing: that all **of the hints are actually effective, and they will also be for you**.

The proof is in the pudding!

PART 1

Thirty Hints for Summer Clothing

Summer Clothing

One of the first things to say about summer clothing is that—contrary to what some may assume—**it can easily allow you to look thinner** while enhancing your strong points, thanks to the fact that **bare legs and arms always have a slimming effect on the whole body**.

Also, there is another element that, surprisingly enough, can flatter your figure while lengthening your body: the fact that in summer, when you get tanned, **you can make extensive use of light-colored garments (white above all)**. As we will see in the next pages, indeed, when the skin is bronzed (even if only slight bronzed), wearing white or light-colored items can flatter the silhouette. This is because having a contrast in color (white dress on a tan leg) will **make your legs look comparatively slimmer and more elongated, enhancing the whole figure**.

Conversely, **wearing dark colors in summer does not have that slimming result that is easily obtained in winter**. Instead, they have the disadvantage of making you look pale while reducing the nice effect of the tan. This makes the legs look shorter and bulkier, highlighting any imperfections (the photos in tip 17 make it clear at first glance).

So if you're used to getting dressed in dark garments "because they have a slimming effect," well, in summer you have to **overcome this concept and change your mindset**: your reward will be **lovely results**.

Still on the subject of the slimming effect of bare skin, you will see how, in many cases, merely **adjusting the hem to a different height** can allow you to achieve a much better result—even a few inches of ankle "in plain sight" can make a difference and make your legs look so much longer and slimmer.

Another thing to consider carefully is the choice of **footwear**. Even in this area, it's better to **avoid dark colors**, and do you know why? Because a dark shoe—especially if the design is not a "minimalist" one—will have a slimming effect only on the shoe itself, *not* on your legs! The foot, in contrast, seems big, and so do the legs, in the absence of black, opaque tights that can keep you on the safe side in winter, thanks to the fact that they create an uninterrupted shoe-foot-leg line.

For this reason, we suggest you to wear **light-colored shoes and sandals**, taking advantage of the thousands of colors of the spring and summer collections.

One last remark for those who think they are overweight: don't forget that in summer, it's often the case that women who are too skinny have fewer tools to boost themselves! A leg that is excessively thin is not necessarily "nice," as it may look too bony or disproportionate, not to mention that a not-exactly-wide cleavage in summer can't take advantage of those super push-up bras that can be hidden under winter clothes.

If you think you have a few extra pounds, then it may be wiser to turn this fact to your advantage and **choose outfits that allow you to enhance your sensuality**, with the help of the following tips that will help you visually cut off a few pounds.

And these tips will make you feel **beautiful, attractive, and chic** on every occasion, **taking advantage of your curves rather than hiding them**.

1. Avoid high heels with capri pants

One of the most important things to consider if you want to get a visually slimmer figure is the choice of **shoes**. And, quite unexpectedly, to get a skinnier silhouette, shoes **do not necessarily need high heels**, especially in summer.

This consideration is valid mainly with capri pants (pants that are longer than your knee but are not as long as trousers). If you want to wear them, always remember that **the most suitable shoes to look slimmer with capri pants are those with very low heels**—ballet flats especially (as you can see in the picture on the right), but also some flat sandals.

High-heeled shoes must be avoided with this type of garment, because—for an optical effect—**they have the result of making your legs look shorter**, as you can see in the image on the left. The shortening effect is even more noticeable from behind, because **the height of the shoe including the heel is almost higher than that of the calf**, a result that is certainly not slimming (and also not chic at all).

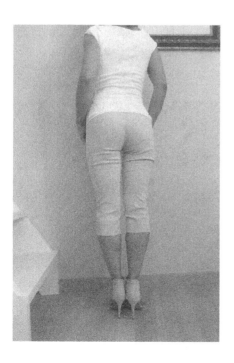 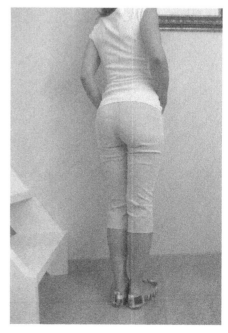

2. Show your ankles with ankle pants

Bare skin, as mentioned at the beginning of this manual, **always has a slimming effect**, whatever your weight and your physical type.

However, if you feel more comfortable with your legs covered, you can use this trick even with long pants, merely adjusting the hem to the ankle or even a bit higher. As **the ankle is the slimmest part of the leg, highlighting it can help you get a slenderizing effect** on the whole figure, as you can see in the image on the right.

On the contrary, **if your ankle is hidden, the whole figure looks less slender**, and the legs look shorter, as you can see in the picture on the left.

As per the shoes, **with ankle-length trousers, you can wear either high heels or flat shoes**; the effect will always be chic and elegant, but pay attention to the model of the shoe itself, and avoid those with ankle straps (see next page).

3. ...but don't pair them with ankle-strap shoes

Still on the topic of ankle-length trousers, keep in mind that to get a slimming effect, you need to **match them with shoes that do not have ankle straps**, as mentioned before. Why? Because **the multiple gaps created by strap-ankle-trousers enlarges your figure** and makes your legs look shorter, even with a high heel, as you can see in the image on the left. (*Note that the hem height is just the same as the photo on the right in tip 2: yes, just where the leg seemed slimmer even with the ballerina flats! Check with a ruler if you do not believe it*). **If you want to wear shoes with an ankle strap, it's better to hem your pants a few centimeters longer,** as in the image on the right, in order to hide the strap itself, so you can create a leaner, continuous line that makes your leg look longer, slimming your figure.

Otherwise, you can wear pants of a shade similar to your skin tone; this eliminates the gap between ankle and trousers, and the strap can still stay in plain sight.

4. Go monochrome

If you wish to make your silhouette thinner and taller, it's better to **avoid using contrasting colors for your upper and lower body**, because this would divide your figure in two, and you would look shorter. **This tip is true especially in the summer**; in winter, in fact, you can easily create an uninterrupted vertical line with stockings and shoes of the same tone, whereas in the summertime, you can't take advantage of that. With summer outfits, indeed, there are many more breakpoints (shoe, leg, shorts, T-shirt), so the best choice is to **choose items of the same color (or at least in hues that are quite similar)**. As you can see below, on the left the stark contrast between shorts and shirt makes the figure look fuller and shorter. Conversely, on the right the choice of **colors that are not necessarily identical but have the same tone** (as well as the ballet flats of a similar tone to the skin) **makes the silhouette look slimmer**.

 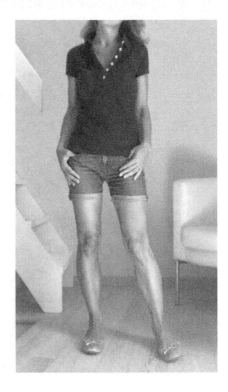

5. Go white

Still on the subject of colors, you can **make the most of the slimming effect** of a monochrome outfit **with an all-white choice**. As we have mentioned above—and as is clear from the images below—using contrasting colors for the upper and lower body makes the figure look shorter. This consideration is particularly true with **a top whose color is in tone with your skin,** which has the effect of **making your bust and waist bigger, making the legs shorter,** also with high heels.

Instead, **an all-white outfit** with a belt that has the same hue as the skin flattens the silhouette and **gives the appearance of a thinner figure**. Thanks to the bronzed skin, the legs and arms look thinner, while the contrast with the white garments makes the whole silhouette look even slimmer.

Moreover, wearing all white is undeniably a timeless classic outfit, always classy, chic, and up to date.

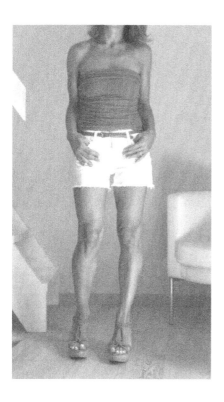 

6. Skirt length: Avoid half measures—Part 1

Now on to summer skirts: the most important thing to remember is that, if you want to get a slender silhouette, you should, first of all, **avoid a half-measure length**, which means that you should wear knee-length skirts (or, on the opposite extreme, miniskirts, as we will see in a while), **avoiding skirts whose hem hits a few inches above the knee**.

The reasons are many. First, **the knee is often the most "difficult" area of the leg**, and if you hem your skirt just a few inches above it, this will end up pointing it out. Second, as you can see in the image on the left, **a hem that comes to mid-thigh may not be the most suitable choice if you want to make your legs look longer**. For these reasons it is **preferable to wear knee-length skirts**, which, especially when combined with heels, **hide the actual length of your legs, making them look longer**, as you can see from the comparison of the images below.

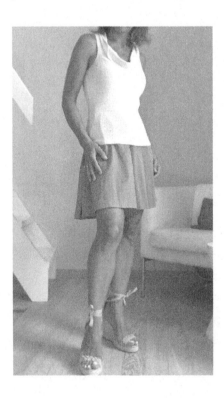 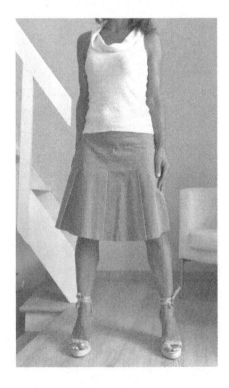

7. Skirt length: Avoid half-measures—Part 2

As we saw on the previous page, for skirts and dresses, the "half-measures" hems (such as in the image on the left) are not the better choice if you want to look slimmer, taller, or thinner.

An alternative to knee-length skirts seen in tip 6 is their exact opposite: **miniskirts, but only if they are "unquestionably mini,"** as in the picture on the right.

That's because **miniskirts, even if placing your knee in plain sight, just leave it unnoticed** (conversely, skirts whose hems end up only a few inches above your knee highlight any imperfections). Besides, **miniskirts help to make your legs look longer** (as there's more leg to see) **and thinner, especially if you are wearing an A-line pattern**, while conversely, too-tight patterns can make your legs appear shorter. And among other things, as we will see in a few pages, A-line miniskirts keep their slimming effect even with ballerina flats.

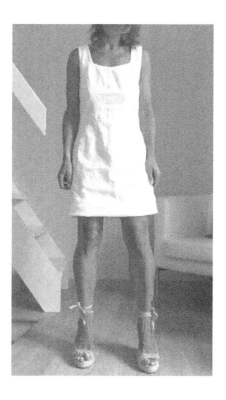
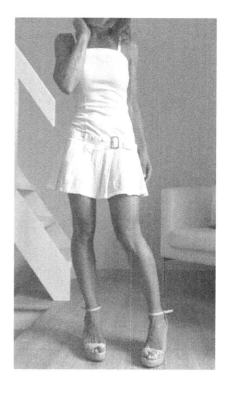

8. How to hide waist and hips—Part 1

An effective way to hide a few pounds around your waist or your hips is to make use of **straight tunics**, as long as they come to **mid-thigh** and you **match them to knee-length pants**.

In fact, thanks to optical proportions between the garments, this outfit leaves the hips and thighs unseen, while the legs, being partly covered, can seem longer than they actually are.

To achieve the best result, however, **it is essential that the pants reach the knee** (or, if you prefer, they can be just a few inches longer) **and that the shirt completely covers the hips**, reaching to mid-thigh.

As you can clearly see from the comparison of the images below, in the picture on the right, the figure looks slim, and the silhouette looks leaner, while in the picture on the left, the legs look shorter, and the hips look wider.

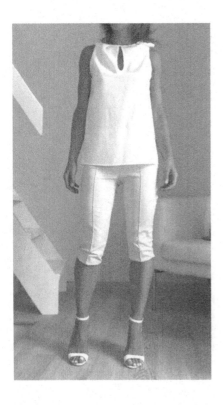 

9. How to hide waist and hips—Part 2

Still on the subject of visually reducing waist and hips with straight tunics, always remember that, as we mentioned above, **if you want an optimal result, you must match them to knee-length pants**.

In fact, the **knee length trousers hide the real length of your leg,** which "goes into the background" and remains unnoticed. Conversely, **ankle pants give "visual" importance to the legs, which, being cut halfway through the tunic, seem much shorter** than they are.

As you can see in the pictures below, in the image on the right, the figure is slender, while in the pictures in the center and on the left the length of the trouser highlights the leg, which seems short because of the length of the tunic.

This "shortening" effect remains the same even if you choose a dark color for the trousers (which makes the leg thinner but increases the "short leg" effect due to the contrasting colors), as well as with a lighter color (which makes the leg look comparatively bigger).

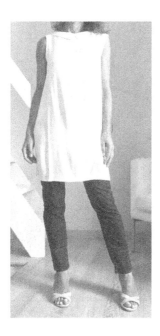  

10. Mini-dresses: Focus on quality

As we will also mention when talking about tops and T-shirts, clothes made with **cheap fabrics** can highlight any imperfection and **add some unpleasant bulges to your silhouette right where you don't need them**. This fact is particularly true with **formfitting mini-dresses**, which, if not properly designed and sewn, can give you some extra pounds **highlighting every inch of your body and making your figure shorter**, as you can clearly see in the picture on the left.

The solution? Choose items that smooth bulges, like the one in the image on the right, picking up **quality fabrics and cuts that help you lengthen your figure** and, among other things, are so much more pleasant to wear.

The difference, as you can see below, is unmistakable: on the left, the poor fabric shows every inch out of place, and on the right, the lovely fabric and the careful cut is definitely flattering, slimming, and generally much more elegant and chic!

11. Pair mini-dresses with flats

As mentioned a few pages ago, mini-dresses and **miniskirts can make your legs look longer and slimmer**, mainly if you avoid formfitting patterns and prefer shapes quite loose at the bottom. What is less known is that **you can obtain this slimming effect also if you pair these items with flat shoes** (be they sandals or ballerina flats). In particular, from a "rear view," some high-heeled shoes can enlarge and widen the leg, due to the fact that when your feet are partially covered, your legs can look shorter (as you can see on the left). Conversely, **ballerina flats paired with a short, wide skirt give your legs a tapered appearance**, minimizing any imperfections. Why does this happen? Because, if you do not have long legs, high-heeled shoes can make your legs look even shorter, due to the disproportion between the height of the shoe and the length of the calf, while **the ballerina flats paired with miniskirts—which lengthen the legs—**flatter your figure, due to the **more proportionate effect**.

12. Take advantage of the striped shirts—Part 1

The striped shirt—also called a "Breton shirt"—is not only a classic item, particularly suitable for summer months, but also **allows to play with different colors** (even with those less suitable to your skin tones) and **can help you make your figure look slimmer and leaner**. How does this happen?

The reason is quite simple and, let's say, quite "geometric": you just have to match a striped shirt with trousers that have one of the colors of the stripes to obtain the lovely effect of visually stretching your whole figure.

This outcome is entirely unexpected because—as we all know and as we will see in a while—using contrasting colors usually adds some pounds to the silhouette.

But with stripes it's different!

As you can see in the pictures below, you can obtain a slimming effect with either a white-and-black striped shirt (center image) or lively colors *(right)*. Instead, **pairing a solid color shirt with pants in a contrasting color *(left)* makes the figure seem fuller**. (Just remember that the effect is better when stripes are wide enough to be perceived even at some distance).

13. Unbutton your polo shirt

In summer a very popular garment is, without doubt, the **polo shirt**. This item is suitable for different styles and, if carefully paired, it can be appropriate on many occasions. However, **in order to boost your femininity**—and highlight your face as well—whatever your size and weight, **you should choose** from close-fitting and slimming patterns with **a slight hourglass shape that optically narrow the waistline**, helping to hide a few pounds because they're **shaped, but not entirely formfitting**. Another key hint for slimming is also to choose a pattern with **a deep neckline** and **wear it with all buttons unbuttoned** (or nearly all of them). Bare skin, as we have said many times, helps to slim the figure, and wearing a V-neck top is one of the simplest ways to look slimmer and taller. Therefore, avoid straight boyfriend patterns with just three spare buttons (like below on the left); they enlarge the upper part of your body and make your figure look fuller. Go for the five-to-seven-buttons patterns, leaving nearly all buttons open, as in the picture on the right.

14. Avoid mid-thigh shorts

Similarly to what we have seen for skirts and miniskirts, if you want to look slimmer and thinner while enhancing the shape of your legs, yet another help comes from **choosing the correct length of your shorts and Bermuda shorts**.

Like it happens for skirts, also with shorts **a mid-thigh length** (as you can see on the left) **is usually the worst choice**. Conversely, if you choose knee-length trousers (image on the right) or pants that are decidedly short (see next page), they can make your figure seem taller.

As you can clearly see in the pictures, the mid-thigh pattern can make your thighs look fuller while highlighting your knees, and your hips and legs look larger than they really are.

On the contrary, **if you lower the hem of your Bermuda shorts to your knees, the leg looks slimmer and longer**.

A difference of a few inches can be enough: sometimes just by lowering the hem of your Bermudas by a couple of inches, you can get an excellent result.

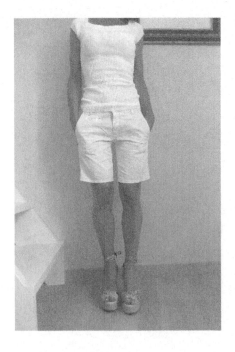 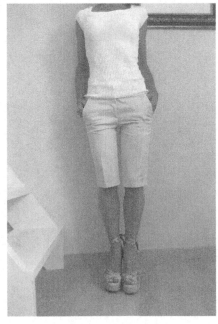

15. Shorten your shorts

As explained on the previous page, **mid-thigh lengths usually do not help to make the legs looking longer**. So if you like to wear shorts (which in summer are suitable for all ages and body types and can be appropriate on several occasions), then it's better to **opt for a very short pattern**.

As described for miniskirts, in the same way, **shorts help you look taller and thinner, adding a few inches to your legs**, while mid-thigh-length trousers make the legs (and the whole figure) fuller. As you can see in the two images below, **with the "really short shorts"** (image on the right), **the leg looks longer and the figure looks slimmer** than the figure on the left. The knee, even if uncovered, is not highlighted, and any imperfections can easily pass unnoticed.

And besides, unlike the Bermudas on the previous page, which, to maximize their slimming effect, require at least a medium-heeled shoe, you can wear **shorts with ballet flats** or low-heeled sandals with an excellent outcome.

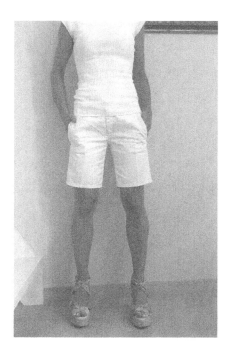 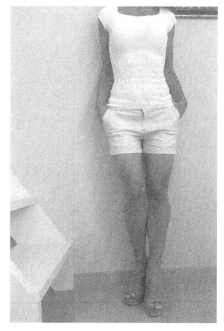

16. Wear low-cut, knee-length dresses

In summer, wearing a dress—especially white, but at least light-colored—**is one of the best choices,** because you don't need to guess out how to pair it, and besides, it makes you feel cool and chic, helping to **hide any imperfections, which, with the right pattern, can become completely invisible**. For the best results, however, it is essential to know how to choose the pattern most suitable to your physique; so if you want to look slender, the first thing to remember is that **sleeveless dresses are definitely better**. Conversely, it's better to avoid those with sleeves (even short sleeves) because, if you are not tall, they enlarge not only the upper part of your body but also your whole figure.

The same applies to clothes that come to just a few inches above the knee (like in the image on the left), which—as seen in the previous pages—shortens the legs and should, therefore, be avoided. The most flattering pattern to wear is in the image below on the right: **low-cut, with a wide, knee-length skirt**.

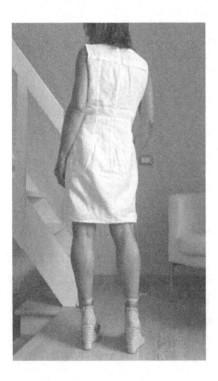 

17. Wear white, A-line dresses

As mentioned at the beginning of Part 1 of the book, when you are already a bit tanned, a tip that always has a lovely outcome—and which, among other things, is suitable for different physical types and on many occasions—is to **make extensive use of white dresses**, which can be chosen in the pattern, style and fabric most appropriate for you. As you can see in the image on the left, **a short, dark dress highlights any imperfections of your legs and makes them look fuller**, especially if the fabric is cheap. Conversely, **a white dress**, better if sleeveless and low-cut, **draws attention to itself, distracting it entirely from the rest of the body, which in comparison will appear slimmer**, while at the same time sensual in a very chic way. The pattern may be short (as in the picture on the right), knee-length (or longer), or with a diagonal line, provided that it is always **loose enough in its lower part** and preferably made of **fresh, natural fabrics** (linen, cotton, silk, viscose).

18. Avoid highly structured dresses

Continuing on the subject of dresses, **a pattern that is highly flattering** and suitable for many body shapes is the one that **combines a shaped line in the upper part of your body with a wider line in the lower part**, which generally makes legs look slimmer, meanwhile completely hiding hips and thighs. However, it's necessary to **pay attention to the number and position of the seams**, which can actually completely change the effect of two otherwise similar garments. Remember that **the greater the number of seams, the greater the amount of fabric** used for the dress, which can visually add some extra weight, as you can see below on the left (the two photos were taken one after the other, and I did not put slimming underwear under the dark-blue dress). The two patterns are quite similar indeed, but the dress on the right has a slimming effect, while the one on the left makes the figure seem fuller because it has too many seams and **too much fabric, which adds some extra pounds**.

19. Be careful with fancy fabrics

For dresses, as well as for other garments, the use of fancy fabrics should be carefully thought out because **some prints undoubtedly can widen your shape**.

Polka dots can be fine—but only if they are large enough, well-spaced, and arranged irregularly, like those in the picture in the center—as can some classical checked or tartan prints. **It's better to avoid prints that create a "messy" effect** as they will likely add extra pounds to your figure. For example, the dress that you can see in the photo on the left, though having a line that usually slims the silhouette, has no flattering effect at all, while the other two are surely more flattering.

Also, consider that in this case more than in others, **it is best to choose quality garments**. This is because to produce fabrics with prints—unless the print is a simple polka dot—is usually more expensive than producing the same fabric in solid color, for the simple reason that there must be someone who creates that print. So it is difficult to find cheap garments with cute, flattering prints, whereas high-quality items generally guarantee better outcomes.

20. Avoid wide, short tops

The length of the top/shirt/T-shirt can do a lot to make the silhouette slimmer and longer.

In particular, if you want to wear a **wide top**, it's better to **pair it with slightly formfitting trousers**, because wearing wide pants will enlarge the whole figure.

Besides, you can obtain better results with a top **long enough to completely (or almost completely) cover the buttocks**.

The fact is that if **your hips are covered, your legs seem to extend** far up to some indefinite point, because the blouse hides the real length of your legs; this provides a slimming effect, as you can see in the image on the right.

Conversely, **wearing wide, short tops makes the silhouette seem bulkier** because, as you can see in the image on the left, the hips are highlighted, and the whole figure looks shorter and larger, even if you do not have any extra pounds.

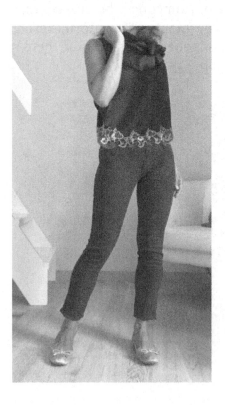 

21. Show some skin around your neck

Continuing on the subject of tops and T-shirts, don't forget that **showing some skin always has a slimming effect**. For this reason, it's better to **avoid items that cover both your shoulders and your neckline** because they enlarge your whole figure, not only the upper part of your body (as you can see in the image on the left). The alternatives can be many; garments with a deep neckline are known to slim the silhouette, but if a deep neckline does not work for you, you can choose tops that **leave your arms and shoulders totally uncovered** (as in the center and right images). These patterns, among other things, are some of the latest trends, so if they are "your style," you'd better take advantage of them, because now you can find them in endless colors, fabrics, and cuts. Besides, they are particularly recommended because they also allow you to move from an informal look to a more elegant one just by changing a couple of accessories. And if you want a sexy look, you can choose a keyhole top like the one in the middle picture that can make you look **sensual while remaining unquestionably chic**.

22. Tops: Avoid cheap fabrics...

Still on the subject of tops and T-shirts, another key suggestion to look slimmer is to **avoid cheap fabrics**, and particularly jerseys, like the one you can see in the picture on the left (unless you can pick out a very high-quality jersey, which is not always easy to find). Cheap, synthetic fabrics, are not the most appropriate choice in the summertime because they are not breathable and can transform the most sophisticated lady into a survivor of the Crossing of the Sahara Desert within minutes. Besides, they have the drawback of **pointing out any imperfections you may have and also those that you *don't* have**, adding unpleasant bulges even to a physique with no extra fat at all.

It is worth to spend a few more dollars to buy garments made with **fabrics of higher quality** that allow you to **achieve a flawless, flattering look**, as you can see in the image on the right.

And if you have maxed out your credit card and still need to buy a top for next Sunday's dinner, a good choice is a crepe top, which guarantees a much better fit and can be bought at a very low price.

23. ...and carefully choose their colors

Another thing to remember in summer is that **cotton clothes**, though comfortable and breathable, **easily lose their color, and this drawback is more obvious in the summertime** because the sunlight itself—as well as frequent washings—may result in a quick fading of the tone of cotton garments. So it's best to **avoid dark colors** (**especially for the day**, in particular for those items that you wash more frequently, like tops and shirts), **giving preference to light colors, white above all**. The perks are many, indeed: on the one hand—as explained in the previous pages—**if you are tanned, white can help you look more slender**, because bronzed skin gives the impression of slimmer legs and arms, and if you are wearing white clothes, this effect is increased. Moreover, thanks to the fact that it reflects the sunlight, white makes many imperfections less visible (conversely, dark fabrics, if they are low quality, when illuminated by the sunlight, add bulk to your figure, as shown in the picture on the left in the previous page). Moreover, lighter-colored garments **do not lose their color,** allowing you to achieve a **chic, polished look**.

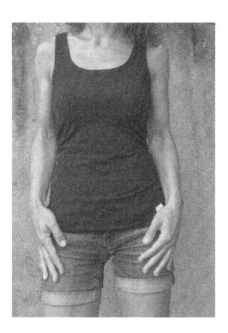 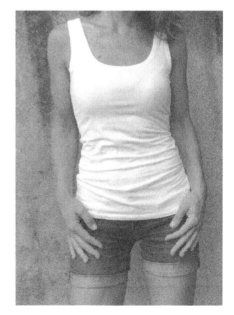

24. Choose minimalist stiletto sandals

Shoes, as every woman well knows, are a key factor if you want a taller-appearing silhouette.

Shoes with **high heels, and in a color that is similar to your skin tone, help you reach your goal** instantly, **whereas dark shoes are known to make the leg seem shorter** (as you can see in the picture on the left).

Anyway, interestingly enough, this is not always the case. If you want to lengthen your legs, indeed, **choosing high heels in a nude color may not be enough**; as you can see in the picture in the center, a nude high-heeled shoe can be not flattering at all.

The reason of this not-so-thinning outcome lies in the "design" of the shoe. **Thin heels are more flattering** than thick heels, **and minimalist shoes**—which, in summer, means sandals with just a few narrow straps—**work far better than shoes that partly cover your feet**. The lower the number and the width of the straps, the more your leg will look slim and narrow.

Showing some skin, as we have frequently pointed out, always has a slimming effect, and this is true also for shoes: a minimalist black stiletto sandal can lengthen your legs more than nude pumps that partially cover your feet and have a chunky heel.

25. Make the most of your accessories

Appropriate use of accessories, especially **belts, can help you enhance your figure** a lot: not only can they help you achieve a more elegant appearance, but with proper use, they can also slim your shape. **This hint is particularly true if you are short** and like to wear knee-length dresses, because with those garments **the use of a belt can be essential for those who would like to look taller** or have longer, thinner-looking legs. **Covering your upper (or middle) body** with wide clothes can actually help hide some extra pounds, but this **works only if you have very thin legs** that are long enough to show them off. Conversely, those of us who are short can get terrible results with garments that are wide around the waistline, as you can see in the image on the left (and I did *not* eat an elephant before taking that picture, I swear it). **If you want to slim your figure and achieve a thinner silhouette, it's enough to highlight the waistline with a belt.** This tip works better if the belt is in tone with your shoes and **contrasts with the dress** (you can wear the belt just above your real waist to lengthen your legs). You can also choose a bright color for the belt (on the right); it catches the eye, so even if you have a few extra pounds around your waist, they go unnoticed.

26. Wear high-waisted trousers...

Wearing **high-waisted, straight pants and pairing them with high-heeled shoes** always has a positive effect on your silhouette, because the slimming effect of the high-waisted trousers is enhanced by the **heel remaining hidden under the pants**. This choice allows you to wear heels as high as you like, because any possible lack of proportion between the height of the heel and the length of your leg entirely disappears, while **the slimming effect of the heel is maximized**. To get the most of this hint, though, be sure to pick out trousers that are quite tight on the hips, and **wear them with a formfitting blouse (or wear the blouse inside the pants)**, so that the waistline remains in sight. As you can see in the pictures below, when the waistline is hidden (photo on the left), the loose line of the blouse adds pounds to the hips and visually divides your body in two while shortening your legs. On the right, the high-waisted pants enhance the silhouette, and the legs look longer and leaner.

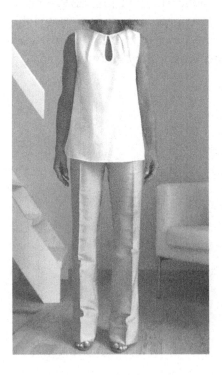 

27. ...and pair them with the right shoes

To get the most out of the slimming effect of high-waisted trousers, it's important to **pay attention to your choice of shoes**, because, as explained above, they must be completely hidden under the trousers. This means on one hand that you can choose the footwear style that you prefer, and a heel as high as you want, due to the fact that the shoe is entirely covered. But on the other hand, remember that **the sole under the toe must be very thin (maximum a few millimeters**, as in the picture on the right). As you can see below, **if you choose shoes with a thick sole (not to mention the platform)**, as on the left, the overall effect would be completely altered: **the figure looks shorter despite a very high heel** (yes, the shoe on the left has a six-inch heel, whereas the one on the right is just three and a half inches), and the pants lose the straight line that helps you achieve the impression of a taller figure. The figure on the right instead is slimmer, besides being much more chic and classy!

 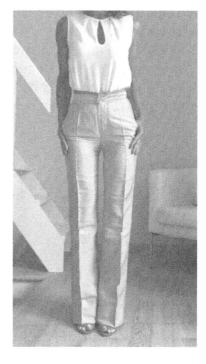

28. How to choose ankle-strap sandals

When choosing summer footwear, another key element not to underestimate is the presence (or not) of **ankle straps** and **their exact width and position**.

Why? Because the position and thickness of straps can completely change the effect of a sandal on the shape of your leg (as well as being a factor that can determine if a sandal is more informal or more elegant).

The main difference is **whether the strap is fastened *over* the ankle bones (malleolus) or *under* them**.

In the first case (**strap fastened right above the ankle bones**, as in the image on the right), **the leg looks slimmer and thinner, because the strap highlights the thinnest part of your leg** (this, of course, works better if you choose minimalist sandals, as seen in tip 24). The drawback is that this kind of shoe is less comfortable for walking.

Conversely, **the strap under the ankle bones** (or even lower on the foot, as in the left and center images) **has the effect of widening the leg,** and for that reason, it's more suitable for those who have very thin calves.

Besides, this kind of footwear is more comfortable because it gives more stability to your foot even in the presence of a heel. So if you want to minimize its widening effect, you can **choose it in a color similar to your skin tone**.

29. How to choose slimming dresses

Another strategic element that can help you slim your figure and make your silhouette slender is to **choose dresses that follow and enhance your shape while not being excessively formfitting** or tight. To quote a phrase that I love very much, "a dress should be tight enough to show that you are a woman, but loose enough to prove that you are a lady" (Edith Head).

This is especially true for those more "formal" dresses that many of us wear only when the dress code strictly requires it and, for that reason, not so easy to pick out. In this case, the hint is to **avoid dresses that are too elaborate as well as items that are too tight**—not only do they highlight any imperfections, they also make your legs look shorter and wider.

As you can see below, in the picture on the left, the legs look bulky, with an unflattering effect, while in the center **the legs look slimmer thanks to the wide line of the skirt**. Furthermore, if you add a belt in a contrasting color (*right*), you can easily achieve a flawless appearance because **the belt catches the attention, drawing it away from any imperfections**.

30. Lingerie and swimming suits—Some hints

In summer **the choice of the right lingerie is essential** to slimming and lengthening your body, as summer garments let people easily glimpse what one is wearing underneath them, due to the use of light-colored, thin fabrics. For these reasons, the best choice in summer is **smooth lingerie, with no lace** (for romantic evenings you can choose items with just a few lace details, with the main part remaining smooth and plain), and **colors similar to your skin tone**; and if you do not like the classic nude tone (which, by the way, is totally understandable), remember that **you can use many other shades that are slightly lighter or darker than your skin tone**, so that they remain unnoticed under your clothes. Another important point to remember— which works for any season—is that, if you are one of the small-busted girls out there (like I am), **wearing a padded bra always helps to slim the waistline**, giving the impression of a thinner waist.

On the subject of **bathing suits**, if you want to enhance your silhouette, it is better to **wear striking colors** (which can also mean white, if your skin is deeply tanned). On the contrary to what was seen above on the subject of the underwear, **the color of a bathing suit should strongly contrast with your skin tone**. And when you get tanned, remember that cool colors like blue and green work better than warm tones because the contrast between the warm hue of your skin and the cool tonality of the bathing suit **helps to achieve a more defined silhouette**. Remember, **intense colors draw attention to the fabric and distract from any imperfection you may have**! For the same reason, it is better to avoid small prints that, seen from a distance, have a confused effect: **if the bathing suit does not stand out, any imperfection is highlighted**! Years ago I made the big mistake of buying a beige and pink-striped bikini; it was so lovely in the shop, but when seen from a certain distance, it became the same color as my skin—a terrible result indeed; besides making me look naked, it gave me a good few extra pounds.

PART 2

Thirty Hints for Spring and Autumn

Spring and Autumn Clothing

In this chapter, we will cover some useful guidelines to feel comfortable, slender, and beautiful in spring and autumn—that is to say, those months when, for climatic reasons, you never know which clothing will be the most appropriate.

Spring and autumn, indeed, **require greater attention to the choice and pairing of clothing items** as well as **a deeper customization**. Why? Because on one hand, **you can't take advantage of the slimming effect of bare skin** (which you can use in summer, as we have seen in Part 1). And on the other hand, you also don't have the option of creating a long, uninterrupted line like you have in winter, when garments cover your body almost entirely (if you did, you would wind up looking odd and unpleasantly overdressed).

Besides, these periods are characterized by the presence of a type of **garment that is not always easy to choose**: I'm talking about **light overcoats and jackets**, whose most popular model is usually not flattering for those who would like to look taller or thinner.

For this reasons, you can make use of **some useful tips that will help you to look more proportional** even with this garments.

Furthermore, you have to keep in mind that some suggestions can a have slightly different outcome depending **on many variables**, like the shape and length of your legs, the width of your neck, and even **the length of your upper leg in comparison with that of your lower leg**—details that are usually neglected but yet essential when talking about proportions.

Let me tell you one thing that I experimented with directly. I have a friend who wears my size, is as short as I am, and is the same weight as me. Her lower leg, though, is about one inch longer than mine. The outcome is that while I need heels when wearing garments that come to the knee, she doesn't need any, because, thanks to the length of her lower leg, she looks lovely and perfectly proportioned even with very low heels.

Another element that is frequently underestimated is **the width of the shoulders in comparison with the length of the legs**. Many people assume that by widening the shoulders, you can make the hips look comparatively thinner, and sometimes this is true. But **this is not the case if you are short-statured**, because **adding volume at the shoulders can have the unpleasant outcome of widening your whole body**.

The variables, as you can see, are infinite.

For this reason, it is always essential that you carefully try every hint to **identify the ones that suit you the best, those that help you enhance your figure the most**.

Thus you will be able to feel slimmer, attractive, and gorgeous immediately, no matter what the place and occasion.

31. Show your ankles

As explained for summer clothing, one of the tricks to slim the figure even with sneakers and flats is to choose **trousers with a close fit (but not too tight)** and **adjust the hem so as to show your ankle**. As already pointed out also in Part 1 of the book, as the ankle is the slimmest part of your leg, **highlighting it has a slenderizing overall effect on your whole figure**, including hips and thighs!

As you can see from the comparison of the pictures below, on the left, the legs of the pants are too wide and too long, and the trousers partially cover the shoes, making the legs look fuller. On the right, the **tapered (but not skinny) legs of the pants give the impression of a slender silhouette**, and the hem adjusted slightly above the ankle helps **slim the whole silhouette because the thighs look slimmer, and so do the hips**. In the photo below, there is also an additional slenderizing effect due to the careful use of the striped shirt, which—as noted in Part 1 (tip 12), and as we also will come across in a few pages—is always useful for lengthening the figure.

32. Avoid short jackets—Part 1

In spring and autumn, a fundamental element of the wardrobe is a **lightweight jacket, whose model and length can have key importance if you want to look thinner** or if you wish to lengthen your legs.

The first thing to point out is that **the most popular model**, the one that reaches just a few inches above the hips, **is absolutely the less flattering one** for those who do not have long legs. In addition to swelling the bust (even with tight models), it enlarges the buttocks and makes the figure stocky while shortening your legs, as you can see in the picture below on the left. **If you want to lengthen your silhouette** and elongate the line of your legs, a total knockout can be obtained with **garments that end just under the buttocks** (as in the image on the right): this outfit **does not point out the actual length of the leg, which therefore seems longer** and slimmer. The result is even better if the model has a belt like the one below.

33. Avoid short jackets—Part 2

As an alternative to very short jackets—which, as pointed out earlier, enlarge the figure and are therefore not suitable for those who would like to look taller or who would like to camouflage a few extra pounds—another flattering option is a **light coat that ends just above the knee**. These items are suitable both with a belt around the waist (as you can see in the photo on the right) or with a straight line (as we will see in the following pages). This garment, which has a slimming effect when combined with high-heeled shoes, **can still look nice even with flats or sneakers**, like the ones you see below.

The important thing, in this case, is that the coat must end just above the knee; with longer models, in fact, the legs would seem shorter, and the whole figure would look stocky. Another trick is to combine it with white or light-colored sneakers (worn without socks or with very thin socks) that will also have a slimming effect on the legs.

34. Take advantage of the striped shirts—2

Similarly to what we have seen for summer clothing (see point 12), an easy way to look slimmer is to **take advantage of the striped shirt**. This item, when paired with the right garments, **can create an unexpected stretching effect** despite the presence of those horizontal lines and contrasting colors that generally have a not-so-flawless outcome.

The best way to wear striped shirts is to **match them with pants that have the *exact* tone of one of the colors of the shirt:** this will visually **lengthen your whole body.** (Be careful: the color must be *identical*, otherwise the effect will be lost. To be on the safe side, choose a striped pattern that contains at least one classic hue, like blue, black, or white). As you can see in the photos, on the left, jeans with a hue different from the blue of the shirt makes the legs look shorter even while wearing a five-inch heel (this was shown also in the left picture in tip 31, where Benedetta is wearing sneakers). **In the picture on the right, instead, the figure appears slender even with sneakers.**

35. Pay attention to back pants pockets

Another important but often underestimated thing to consider, if you want to flatter your figure, is paying very close attention to back pants pockets. Their **position, shape, and seams can give the impression of a larger derriere**, or conversely can slenderize your hips, creating the impression of a slimmer figure. **Large pockets, or pockets that are too low** (such as those in the photo on the left), **give the impression of a bigger behind** while at the same time making the legs look shorter and bulkier. Moreover, the hips look wider and the buttocks less toned.

Instead, wearing **shaping trousers without pockets** as in the image on the right **can flatter your figure with a slimming effect**. The only obstacle is that it is not always easy to find in stores jeans without back pockets, so as an alternative, you can choose **garments with back pockets that are not too big**. This tip works best when the seams are the same color as the fabric. Otherwise, you can make use of **stretch cotton pants** like the ones below on the right, **which can be as comfortable as jeans**.

 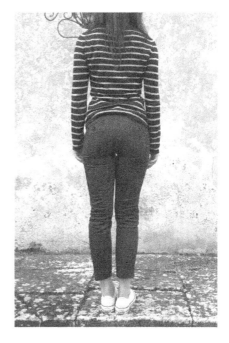

36. Which overcoat should be worn with a skirt?

As we encountered a few pages ago, in spring and autumn, **overcoats are a must-wear of the season**. Besides, **if you choose high-quality fabrics, they can provide a more refined and chic look** even when the rest of the outfit consists mainly of basic garments (such as jeans and T-shirt). It is therefore essential to know the pattern that can help you to get the most of your strong points while hiding what you want to keep hidden. That being said, always remember that for those who want to look slimmer, the best solution is to **choose an overcoat with the belt, especially when matching the overcoat with a dress or a skirt**. As you can see below, a straight pattern (on the left) enlarges the figure, while **a model that is more formfitting and also has a belt (on the right) slims the silhouette while stretching the legs**. Hint: the result is better if the color of the overcoat is similar to that of the skirt.

37. Which overcoat should be worn with pants?

Continuing on the subject of overcoats, as mentioned in point 36, **a straight-line overcoat** paired with a skirt or with a dress is not the most flattering option if you want to look thinner or taller, as it requires a tall figure or at least long legs. If you are going to wear an overcoat with a straight line, though, **you can pair it with pants**, but don't forget that in order **to create a vertical line that elongates your figure, it's better to leave it open** (or add a scarf, as in tip 64). More importantly, it is better to choose **pants quite close-fitting (but not too tight),** picking the ones with stretch fabric, **in order to balance the volume of your upper body**. A straight overcoat **can also be matched with capri pants and sandals** (as long as the color of the shoes is similar to your skin tone), as in the image on the right. Thanks to the proportions between these garments, **the silhouette looks proportionate** even with contrasting colors.

38. Wear shaping trousers

Choosing the right pattern for your trousers can always help you visually cut off a few pounds while slimming and harmonizing your shape in just the right places. **This tip is true more than ever when wearing flat shoes** or sneakers. In this case, the most flattering option is to choose **shaping, close-fitting pants,** which can help you **camouflage a few extra pounds**. As you can see from the comparison between the two images, on the left you can clearly see how **large pants have the effect of enlarging your whole body**, because the wide trouser legs enlarges the whole figure while shortening the legs. Conversely, **the trousers on the right, which are shaping but not skinny, elongate the legs** and help the buttocks appear more toned, making the silhouette slimmer. Besides, in this case, **an additional slimming effect is provided by pairing the pants with a top that is exactly the same color**, while on the left, the contrast between the color of the two garments, even if slight, enlarges the figure.

39. Overcoat and pants: Some more hints

Another important feature you particularly need to take to heart when wearing an **overcoat** is that it **hides everything from the knee up while highlighting the lower part of your body**, so you must be particularly careful in choosing which pants to wear, as well as picking out the right shoes to pair them with.

This hint is particularly true if you wear flat shoes or sneakers whose color contrasts with the hue of the pants: in this case, the pattern of the pants—as well as their hem length—should be the ones most suitable for you.

As you can see below on the left, **trousers that are too long** and not appropriately hemmed not only shorten the legs but also **make the whole figure look fuller**. It is enough to **shorten the jeans,** so they come straight to the ankle (as in the picture on the right), **to get a slimmer silhouette** and obtain a totally enjoyable result that makes you look thinner even without wearing high-heeled shoes.

40. Make the most of accessories and details

Accessories and details are a great way to **modify the proportions of your figure**, to help flatter your silhouette; if you give some attention to them, they can easily work to your advantage. In the pictures below, you can see how two similar outfits that mainly consist of short jacket + jeans + sneakers **can have a different outcome if you simply change details**.

In the image on the left, the figure is enlarged, and the legs look shorter.

On the right, the choice of a jacket with a solid color (without those white details that draws attention to the middle) and the white sneakers instead of the darker ones, together with the beige and blue scarf (which matches the colors of the outfit) **elongates the body because it draws attention to the slimmer points of the figure**.

Moreover, this is also emphasized by the white cuffs at the wrists, which make **the arms seem shorter and therefore**, in contrast, make **the legs look longer**.

41. Use contrasts to your advantage—Part 1

If you love using **monochrome items** in your outfit (the classic black and white, as well as grey, beige, and blue) it's essential to learn how you can **emphasize these hues with contrasting colors** and **use them to enhance and compliment your silhouette** by applying some simple geometric rules that can make your figure look longer. The easiest way to play with contrast is to **wear a white or light-colored overcoat open over a dark-colored outfit**. As we mentioned a few pages ago, light-colored overcoats may have the drawback of enlarging the figure, especially when combined with dark jeans, as in the image below on the left. This unpleasant outcome, though, can be wholly modified if you **leave the overcoat unbuttoned over a monochrome dark ensemble**, as you see in the picture on the right (the opposite, meaning a dark overcoat over an outfit in a light color, does not work the same way). When it's too cold to leave the coat open, **you can still get the same outcome adding a long, dark scarf**, as we will see in tip 64.

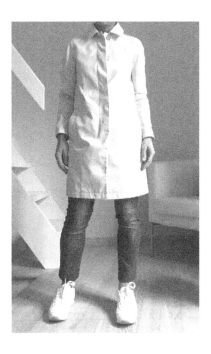 

42. Use contrasts to your advantage—Part 2

Continuing on the subject of contrasts, as mentioned in the previous chapters, choosing **contrasting colors for the upper and lower parts of your body has the drawback of making the figure look shorter**. If you want to look slimmer and taller, therefore, **combinations of contrasting colors should be applied strategically**, so they can help you **lengthen your silhouette instead of shortening it**. For example, if you want to match a light-colored top and dark trousers, you can get a real knockout just by adding a dark jacket, which visually **creates a vertical line that elongates your legs**. As you can see from the comparison between the two images below, on the left the legs appear shorter, while on the right, the continuity between trousers and jacket creates an optical effect that stretches the figure while making the legs look leaner. This solution is better than a totally dark outfit because **the wide line of the jacket is balanced by the thin silhouette of the light-colored top**.

43. ...but with caution

Still on the subject of contrasts, another nice way to take advantage of contrasting colors with an informal look is to wear a **light-colored, loose boyfriend shirt worn open on a darker outfit**.

Just as with overcoats, this ensemble not only **camouflages any extra pounds around waistline and hips**, but it also **creates an uninterrupted vertical, thin line** that flatters the figure while lengthening the silhouette.

Thanks to the stark contrast between the colors, the width of the white shirt does not draw any attention to itself, while **the dark line above it makes your body appear so much longer and slimmer**, as you can see in the image below on the right.

Conversely, a dark shirt worn over a white outfit (as in the picture on the left) does not work the same way; conversely, it's entirely counterproductive, because the white garments stand out of the dark shirt, enlarging the whole figure.

44. Use scarves to slim the silhouette

As we have pointed out many times, one of the main tricks to appear longer and leaner is **avoiding decisive contrasts between your upper and lower body** (or using them strategically).

That being said, **if you want to wear a light-colored sweater together with dark-colored pants**, you can still enhance this ensemble just by **adding a scarf that has a color similar to that of the pants**, because the scarf extends the line of the legs, with an overall slimming effect. The reason lies in the fact that **the eye perceives the clothes much more than your actual figure**. So if you wear a scarf that has the same color as the trousers, you can create the **visual impression of a thin silhouette** that makes your figure slender and harmonious.

As you can see in the pictures below, even with an intensely contrasted outfit like the one on the left, you can quickly get a slim look just by adding **a scarf, which, besides elongating the figure, gives you a chic, refined look**.

45. Wear boot-cut pants

One of the most suitable items to wear if you want to make your legs seem longer and slimmer are **boot-cut trousers** (tight around the leg and knee but looser at the bottom) that are a must-wear for **flattering the silhouette and getting a taller-appearing figure**. This pattern always has the pleasant outcome of harmonizing your form and allows you to take advantage of your curves rather than hide them. Besides, it **allows you to wear shoes with a heel as high as you want**, due to the fact that the heel remains hidden, so you can choose very high heels without worrying about the disproportion between heel and leg.

As you can see from the comparison between the images below, the boot-cut jeans (picture on the right) **make the leg slimmer because the high heel is completely covered**. Conversely, when the heel remains visible (as in the pictures on the left and in the middle) the legs are shortened because of the disproportion between heel and calf (**this rule is crucial with coats coming to the knee**). Some hints to maximize the slimming effect: the color of the pants must be dark, and **the bottom should be wide enough to cover the heel, but no wider**; otherwise it has the unpleasant outcome of widening your leg.

46. Hints to pick out the right dress

Choosing a dress in spring and autumn can be quite hard, because the "show-some-skin" approach that works wonderfully in summer is not so easy to achieve, and the "black-opaque-tights" approach of the winter months can have an unpleasant "overdressed effect" when the weather is not so cold.

Here are some hints to enhance your silhouette no matter what the occasion:

- The classic **sheath dress** is not for everyone: it usually **requires a figure not necessarily lean, but well-proportioned**. For instance, a size 12 with wide breasts and wide hips can be delightfully flattered by a sheath dress, while a wide-busted size 4 isn't; so if your hips are comparatively wider than your bust (or the opposite), you're better choosing other patterns.

- **For the wide-busted ladies** out there, the best choice is usually **a wrap dress,** which **slims your waistline, shaping and highlighting your curves** instead of covering them.

- A pattern with a diagonally cut hem can work the same way as a wrap dress: **asymmetric-bottom garments always add a few inches to your legs** and can be suitable for multiple occasions.

- **The quality of the fabric is a must for formal dresses**: a soft but shaping fabric flatters your figure while slimming the silhouette (and always assures a perfect outcome, making your look classy and chic). Conversely, **a dress made with a poor-quality fabric highlights any imperfections**—even those you *do not* have, as we have seen in tip 22—and therefore it's better to avoid it.

- The choice of **fancy fabrics** always needs some thoughtful considerations. Keep in mind what we saw in tip 19, and remember that if you wish to buy a dress with a fancy fabric, it's better to **be on the safe side and choose the highest quality**, because cheap, fancy garments are unlikely to flatter your body.

47. Pair dresses with stoles

Still on the subject of dresses, don't forget that **for a taller-appearing figure, a shawl**—which can also be a simple scarf like the one we saw in tip 44, large enough and properly worn—**works better than a blazer**. Why? Because, as discussed previously, **combining a blazer with a dress (or skirt) frequently has the unpleasant outcome of enlarging the whole figure**, due to the volume in both the upper and lower body. (So if you want to hide a few extra pounds, a blazer works better with trousers, plus high heels that will add length to your legs). **When wearing a dress**, instead, you can get amazing results by **pairing it with a stole,** which helps you **visually cut off some pounds** and can have an extra-slimming effect because it **brings attention away from your hips or your tummy**, focusing on your cleavage. A hint: **avoid stiff fabrics** and give preference to fabrics such as linen or silk (when it's warmer) or a viscose-wool blend (when it's colder), like in the pic on the right.

48. Wear trench coats

The classic **trench coat is a truly timeless** item that can be suitable for all kinds of body types. Thanks to its line tight around the waist (without being too close-fitting) and wide at the bottom, this garment can enhance your figure, visually extending the silhouette of your legs and **shaping and highlighting your curves** instead of covering them (the result is better when wearing high-heeled shoes). In the meantime, it allows you to **camouflage a few extra pounds around the hips and thighs—** but also, in part, around the waistline—thanks to its particular shape.

To make the most out of this item, though, a few cautions are needed, especially for those who do not have long legs.

First, always **match it with high-heeled or medium-heeled shoes and boot-cut pants**, which, being tight on the knees, can emphasize the slender effect on the legs (avoiding shorter and straight pants like those in the photo on the left).

A second hint is to leave the trench slightly open around your neck, or, when it gets colder, **match it with a scarf in tone with the trousers**. As you can see in the image below on the right, the result is not only slimming but also very chic!

49. ...and match the appropriate shoes

Continuing on the subject of trench coats, although being an item that can be helpful to many of us, in some cases—as previously encountered—they may **require combination with high-heeled shoes**. However, this rule does not apply to everyone: what matters with this garment is not so much your height in itself, but **the relationship between the length of your thigh and that of your calf**, as was also mentioned at the beginning of Part 2 of the book. Let me explain more clearly: a woman whose legs are not so long, but who has longer calves, can also wear a trench coat with sneakers or flats. Conversely, **if you have shorter calves (like I do), high-heeled shoes are almost indispensable**. As you can see in the pictures below, the same trench coat paired with sneakers cuts the figure shorter, but when pairing it with high-heeled pumps, the outcome is totally satisfying (note that the slimming effect is maintained both with shoes that match the color of the trousers as well as with shoes that match the trench coat instead).

Another option is to **match the trench coat to knee-length boots**: as **the boot hides the lower part of the leg**, the length of the leg itself is not highlighted.

50. Carefully pair ultra-skinny trousers

Ultra-skinny pants are very fashionable these days, though, as you can imagine, it's better to make careful use of them because they undoubtedly **highlight any extra pounds around the buttocks and the hips** while shortening the legs.

Generally speaking, **ultra-skinny styles are a must-wear in combination with knee-high boots and with wide and long sweaters**, because they balance the volume of the upper body while having a sort of "sheath" effect. Also, they do not add any volume to the knee, which allows a nice outcome while wearing knee-high boots that are quite tight on the calf. However, **if you are wearing your favorite sneakers, it's always better to pair them with straight pants**, or at least "soft skinny" ones. Why? Because **overly form-fitting trousers can highlight the calves and shorten your legs** even with a dark color (picture on the left), while a silhouette that is close-fitting but not too tight can harmonize your whole figure (picture on the right).

51. Take advantage of bright-colored bags

An effective trick to make your body appear slimmer and to hide what you want to be hidden, **drawing attention away from your midsection and hips**, is to take advantage of **mid-sized, bright-colored bags**.

This hint can easily be applied to any monochrome outfit, with the double advantage of being very easy (and fun) to achieve, while being **suitable for any body type**. This simple trick works wonderfully and can help you get a chic, sophisticated look with no effort. Conversely, **the "all-black" approach, besides being quite boring, has the unpleasant outcome of enlarging the whole figure**. Why? Because a dark bag paired with a similarly dark outfit just adds volume where you do not need it (photo on the left), while a **medium-sized bag** in a vibrant hue (or **in a color that contrasts with that of the outfit**) always has a slimming effect because it **visually takes volume away from your middle**, minimizing any imperfections (hips, waist, height).

52. Wear minimalist heels

As we have pointed out in the Part 1 of the book when talking about summer garments, the mere choice of **high-heeled shoes is not enough to make the legs seem longer and leaner**. And, in the act of extreme injustice, this is particularly true for those of us who are not tall, especially in spring and autumn, when we cannot wear black opaque tights that, when paired with black heels, make a long, vertical line that lengthens the legs.

So, to make the most of the slimming effect of the heels, it is always better to choose **shoes that have quite a "minimalist" style**, which means they leave the feet uncovered as much as possible, in order to take advantage of the slimming effect of the naked skin.

Besides, it's also better to **avoid heels that have a platform.** Why? Because when wearing shoes that partly cover the feet (on the left) or that have a high platform, even if you gain a few inches in height, this goes totally unnoticed, and the legs look quite short (in that case, it would be better to wear sneakers—at least they are more comfortable).

Conversely, **if the shoe is "minimal"** (on the right), **it lengthens the legs, making the whole figure slimmer**.

53. Carefully play with monochrome

Wearing a **dark monochrome outfit** is usually **considered the quickest way to look slimmer**: even those who do not pay attention to their clothing know that to look thinner, it's enough to dress entirely in dark hues, and that's it. However, things are not always so simple. **A monochrome approach does not always work**, because instead of camouflaging some extra pounds, it can sometimes do the opposite. This is mainly true in spring and autumn, when, due to quick temperature changes, it's common to have **an overdressed look, which is not flattering at all**. In this case, remember that **bare arms do not match with dark stockings** (on the left). When in doubt, it's better not to wear any socks (on the right), if you do not want to rush to take them off just as you take off your sweater! Anyway, generally speaking, remember that **a monochrome option can be quite boring and entirely uninteresting,** while using different hues you can achieve a slim, classy, and chic look (see point 51).

54. Match shoes with scarves

Still on the subject of shoes, one of the most common choices is to wear **shoes the color of the pants**, which is considered an easy way to get a slimmer figure. Well, as a matter of fact, **this approach does not always ensure the best result** (as you can see in the picture on the left).

If you want to achieve a slimmer and more harmonious figure, a second, **more exciting option,** which is also **far more stylish,** is to **match a monochrome outfit with shoes in a vivid or bright color**, while adding **a scarf that contains a hue similar to that of the shoes**. This trick works wonderfully because it flatters the figure and **extends the silhouette** thanks to the fact that the eye goes from head to toe, adding length to the body while having a slimming effect. Besides, this outfit is **always chic even with informal garments**, as you can see in the picture on the right. Hint: you can also get this result with a necklace or something else on your upper body, and the color does not necessarily have to be identical, just similar.

55. Unbutton your shirt—Part 1

As encountered in Part 1 of the book, talking about the polo shirt (see tip 13), wearing **garments buttoned to the neck may shorten your figure while making it look fuller**, so it's better to avoid it if you want to look slimmer. In spring and autumn, instead of the summer polo, it's more common to wear button-up shirts, but the rule itself does not change. So when wearing a shirt, always remember to **unbutton the upper buttons**; this way you can easily **create the effect of a V-neck that visually stretches your figure out** and gives you a taller-appearing silhouette. As you can see in the photos below, the buttoned shirt with the long sleeve *(left)* makes the figure look shorter, while the same shirt slightly unbuttoned has the effect of **lifting the breasts while shaping the whole figure**. **This works even better if you shorten the sleeves** of the shirt a little: the arms look shorter, and the legs look comparatively longer. Another slimming detail is the belt contrasting with the pants, which distracts the eye and doesn't add any volume to the waistline.

56. No cuffs with blue jeans!

Traditional blue jeans are undoubtedly a timeless, and classical garment, which **fit almost all styles and sizes**.

Besides, they also have another advantage, which is bound to their particular color.

In fact, denim pants, when chosen in **the classical blue tones, become a perfect neutral base** that, thanks to their typical neutral color—**not too light, not too dark, not too colorful**—can be flawlessly **paired with darker and lighter garments** without creating those stark contrasts between upper and lower body, which, as we have explained, are to be avoided if you want to obtain a slimmer, taller figure.

At the same time, though, it's better to **avoid light-colored jeans, and especially the light-blue ones** (apart from white jeans, as we will see in tip 58), which can have the effect of **widening the legs**, as well as the irregularly faded ones.

Furthermore, one thing that is best to **avoid with dark jeans**—and that is now totally fashionable—is **the "scuff" at the bottom** (instead of a properly sewed hem), which, with blue jeans, is totally unsuitable due to the particular construction of the denim fabric (dark on one side, and clearer on the other).

As a matter of fact, **this difference in the color of the pants** has the unpleasant effect of **breaking and shortening the leg**: so, even if **scuffs can be nice on a long, thin leg**, they don't do any magic for those who have not-so-endless legs, making them appear fuller and shorter.

Incidentally, this does not happen with white jeans or with fabrics that, unlike denim, have the same color on both sides. In these cases, you can do the scuff, but pay attention to be sure that it's sewn with care, which means that the **trouser should not be merely rolled over itself**, but it has to be **properly hemmed** before being turned on itself. The casual wrap gives **the impression that the trouser is too long for the leg that is wearing it**, and besides, it shortens the whole figure, with a totally unfashionable effect.

57. Learn how to hem your pants

As we have mentioned previously, hemming your pants **at the appropriate length is essential to achieve a taller-appearing figure**, because it makes your legs look longer and leaner (picture on the right). Conversely, if you do not properly hem your trousers and leave them just wrapping around your legs like ivy, the whole body looks less slender (picture on the left). This is mainly true **when wearing knee-length coats**, because the lower leg is the only part that remains visible, and **if the trousers are not properly hemmed**, instead of a long, vertical, straight line that visually stretches the silhouette, you get **a messy ensemble that shortens the whole figure**.

The solution? **Learn how to hem your pants yourself**! Ask your mother, or search the web for guidance; it really takes only a few minutes, and besides, it allows you study the effects of the different lengths of the hem at home, rather than relying on a shop assistant who may not know which length is more suitable for you. In addition to saving a few dollars, **it's a great way to get to know what flatters your figure most**!

58. Pay attention to the color of your jeans

As mentioned in tip 56, when picking a pair of jeans, usually you can get the best results **choosing the dark and the medium-dark ones, or the opposite—the white ones**. Conversely, medium-light colors are not the wisest choice if you want to look slimmer or taller, because they give the appearance of a large leg. As you can see from the comparison of the images below, even with the same boot-cut pattern (which is usually slimming thanks to its flared silhouette) and with medium-heeled pumps, **the light-blue jeans enlarge the leg and cut the figure shorter**, while **the dark ones smooth bulges** while lengthening the silhouette. **As per the white ones**, interestingly enough, they have the effect of **harmonizing the body despite their color**; this is due partly to the fact that optical white makes any imperfection less noticeable (thanks to the fact that it reflects the light) and partly to the **continuity of color between shoes and sweater**. One more hint: if you like to wear **jeans in vivid or unusual colors**, don't forget that **it's essential to choose quality fabrics**. When picking out medium-dark or white jeans, you can buy cheap garments because the difference with high-quality ones is minimal, but for brighter hues, the difference is far more visible.

59. Choose flared skirts

In spring and summer, skirts are not so easy to wear, because, as we mentioned when talking about dresses (point 46), we do not have tanned legs as in summer (which enhances the "show-some-skin" approach that is always slimming) and we do not wear black, opaque tights like in winter (which, in combination with dark shoes, create an uninterrupted vertical line that visually stretches the figure). That being said, the first thing to say is that **for occasions that require a formal dress code, it is always better to wear a dress**, which is also an easier way to slim the figure while lengthening the whole body (see points 46–47 for some hints). When you are picking a skirt, which can be the most suitable choice for those who do not love formal clothing, always remember that **a flared silhouette always works better than a straight one**, because **the volume at the bottom balances out hips and legs, harmonizing your whole body** while hiding a few extra pounds (picture on the right). Conversely, **straight skirts** (as on the left) generally **make the legs look shorter** and give the impression of a more full-figured body. If you wish to wear them, pair them with a sleeveless top *(center)* that does not add any extra volume to the silhouette.

60. Avoid bright-colored socks and stockings

A key element for making the legs longer and leaner as well as more proportionate and harmonizing the whole figure is **the proper choice of socks and stockings**, which can help stretch the silhouette of calves and **add length to a short leg**, but which—if not properly chosen—can add some extra pounds, enlarging the figure.

Needless to say, **colorful socks or fancy stockings** (which, among other things, are now totally fashionable) are items that **should be used with extreme caution**. And if you do not have long, thin legs, you should avoid these garments altogether. Not only do they make you look less chic and elegant, but as a matter of fact, they have the unpleasant outcome of **dividing your figure** while drawing attention to themselves and **enlarging your ankles**.

The most flattering solution with sneakers is **not to wear any socks at all, as long as the temperature allows it**, so you can get the most of the slimming effect of showing some skin. When it's colder, you can opt for **knee-high nude socks**. However, they must be really very thin, almost invisible, so your legs look naked. These items keep your feet warm anyway, and besides, being similar to your skin tone, if they happen to tear, this remains almost invisible! Alternatively, I think that fishnet socks and stockings are very nice and suitable for many styles and nearly every body type.

Conversely, **avoid thick knee-high socks** (they always have a horrible effect, not feminine at all), **bright-colored pop socks,** and socks with lively, contrasting prints that always shorten the legs.

More suitable are socks and stockings in tone with the color of the shoe or stockings with delicate tone-on-tone prints, but they must be chosen with great care to avoid unnecessarily widening your legs' circumference.

Hint: stockings with vertical lines works nice for perfectly straight, tapered legs, while if you have large calves, they only highlight them, so it's better to avoid them.

PART 3

Thirty Hints for Winter Clothing

Winter Clothing

Winter clothing is characterized by the presence of two key elements, which by the way are deeply linked to each other: the **outerwear** (coats, quilted jackets, and so on), along with the **style and length of pants and skirts**.

These two aspects are intrinsically related because, in winter, **your lower leg is the only part of your body that remains "in plain sight" when wearing knee-length coats**, so it is essential to use a few hints to make the most of it.

On the subject of the outerwear, the first thing to consider is that many of the people you meet during the day will only see you in your coat; therefore, it's essential to choose the type most suitable for you, if you want to feel beautiful and proportionate even while wearing it.

As for the **length and pattern of pants and skirts**, it's important to **make the right choice not only considering your figure, but also according to the footwear**. In this regard, a useful hint can be buying two identical jeans that fit you perfectly and adjusting their hems at two different heights so that you can pair them both with heels and with sneakers.

Another thing to keep in mind is that **for some garments**—not all, luckily—**the quality of the fabric in winter is crucial**, not only because your clothes must keep you comfortably warm and not get damaged by the snow or the rain, but also because **choosing quality garments is always useful to flatter your**

silhouette, due to the fact that a beautiful fabric and a flattering cut can enhance your figure, whereas a poor-quality one can add unpleasant extra pleats to your body, shortening your figure (and besides, it's not chic at all).

In these cases, therefore, make sure that you do not buy low-quality items.

Buy less, but wisely.

Invest your time in researching for the item that is just perfect for you, instead of buying your twentieth cheap, acrylic black sweater.

And when you need a "therapeutic" purchase (it is always a pleasant way to take care of yourself!), then keep yourself to something harmless. Avoid blazers and jerseys (if they are not high-quality, they lose their shape in minutes) in favor of a sleeveless top or a padded bra—even a cushion for your sofa or a lip pencil can work: something, namely, that **does not affect your wallet and does make you feel pampered without any impact on your style!**

61. Wear contrasting coats

If you are not very tall, a heavy coat may have an enlarging effect, adding inches where you don't want to, because wearing wide garments frequently has the outcome of **shortening the figure** (as you can see in the photo on the left).

To make the most of this item and visually cut off some pounds while slimming your form, it is important to **choose simple A-line patterns, flowy and with a straight cut**, avoiding coats with pleats that may be cute in the window but, when worn, have the drawback of enlarging the whole body.

Besides, it is also better to avoid too-long styles that shorten the legs. Finally, as we will soon see for short jackets (point 64), a useful trick is to **match a coat in a bright color with a monochrome outfit and scarf**, which **visually creates a thin, slender silhouette**. And as the temperature rises, you can unbutton your coat, leaving the scarf to cover your neck and bust (picture on the right).

62. Add a belt to quilted jackets

A quilted jacket is one of the basics of the winter season, both for its practicality and because it warms much more than any other garment that is not a fur coat. This item, however, has the well-known disadvantage of being **a garment that generally is not flattering at all, because it undoubtedly enlarges the silhouette** (picture on the left).

If you want to wear it flawlessly, you should, first of all, **choose a close-fitting pattern**; and furthermore, you can **wear it with a belt** (even if there was no belt when you bought it, **you could always add one**).

The two images below clearly show how **the belt reduces the waist** and makes the whole figure slimmer.

This trick works even if you have a few extra pounds around your waist because the thick fabric of the quilted coat minimizes any imperfections, and **the eye only perceives the hourglass figure created by the belt.**

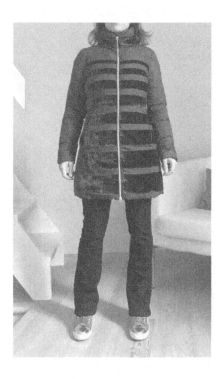 

63. ...and pair them with knee-high boots

Another effective way to wear quilted coats, diminishing their widening effect, is to choose an intermediate length: not too long and not too short. **The ideal length is about mid-thigh** (as in the images below). In fact, for proportional reasons, a quilted jacket that comes to the knee is suitable only for those who are quite tall and have long legs (the long leg balances the excessive volume of the upper part); while a length that is quite short requires some caution, as we will see later. Also, another element that helps to make the figure slimmer is to **pair it with knee boots** and with skinny pants (picture on the right) because **the volume of the upper body is balanced out** by the vertical line created by the skinny pants and the knee-high boots. **This hint works even better if the belt is fastened slightly higher than your actual waist**, giving the impression of long, slender legs. The effect can also be obtained with slightly flared trousers (as on the left), but undoubtedly it's less effective.

64. Make use of scarves with short jackets

As we have encountered both in Part 1 and Part 2 of the book, talking about summer, spring, and autumn clothes, **a low neckline** is a very effective and easy way to make your silhouette look slimmer, because it visually **reduces the proportion of the bust while, in comparison, the legs seem longer and leaner**. In winter, though, wearing garments with a low neckline is not very common, but **you can still take advantage of the slimming effect of a deep neckline making extensive use of scarves** in colors similar to your pants and contrasting to that of the coat. Similarly to what we have seen in point 44, **a scarf whose color contrasts with the tonality of the coat** evokes the effect of the neckline and **visually extends the line of legs**, allowing to **reduce the disproportionate and enlarging effect of short jackets**, as shown from the comparison of the images below. The result is even better if, under the short jacket, you wear a long sweater that comes just below the buttocks (as in the picture on the right), so as to hide the real length of the legs.

65. Choose jackets that cover the buttocks

Contrary to what we have seen for spring and autumn clothing (see point 32) and for mid-thigh quilted coats (point 62) when wearing **short** winter jackets, it is better to **choose patterns that do not have a belt**. What's the reason? Because if the jacket is short, the belt has the effect of **widening the derriere**, due to the fact that a winter jacket has a volume considerably bigger than that of a lightweight jacket.

As to the length of this item, if you want to look slimmer while adding a few inches to the legs you can **choose a jacket that ends just under the buttocks**, as in the picture on the right. **Shorter models** (as on the left), conversely, **can shorten your legs while highlighting the hips.** Besides, similarly to the long sweater seen on the previous page, this length camouflages the real length of the legs, that look longer.

Again, if you do not wear high heels, it is preferable to **balance the bigger volume on the bust with trousers that have close-fitting legs** (but not too tight), so avoid wide-leg pants.

66. How to pair footwear with pants

"The biggest mistake women make is wearing pants that aren't of the right length for their shoes" (Kate Young). In the winter, as we said at the beginning of Part 3, this feature rises to greater importance because, when wearing coats, **the lower half of the leg is the only part of the body that remains in plain sight** and therefore must be flawless.

So let's see the best combinations of footwear and pants in order to slim and harmonize the figure.

Ankle boots are one of the most common items in winter, and undoubtedly, **when worn under the trousers**, they can be suitable for many body types and **in combination with many different garments**.

However, **if, instead of wearing them under the legs of the pants, you wear them over the trousers, then it's better to wear a monochromatic and quite close-fitting outfit**. Why? Because ankle-boots have the effect of visually dividing the legs in two, making them look shorter, so they must be balanced out with items that are not too wide (and for the same reason, it's better to avoid contrasting colors).

When wearing wide trousers, as we have previously found, it is better to **pair them with high heels**, especially if you are not tall (if you are taller, you can wear them even with a medium heel) **in order to minimize their widening effect**.

Besides, remember that **the shoe must remain almost completely hidden under the trousers**; this combination will lengthen your silhouette pleasantly and harmoniously, flattering your figure.

Last but not least, **always avoid shoes with a platform** (not to be confused with wedges) because, besides being neither chic nor elegant, **they cut the figure shorter with any kind of pants** (or skirts). They do not add any length to your legs or your figure. **You will only end up looking like you are standing on a shoebox with your short legs**—not a very flattering result, indeed. So, if you want to look taller and slender, *never* buy them, and *never* wear them.

67. Carefully pair wide sweaters

Wide sweaters are an item not always easy to wear. If not properly paired, they **can give the appearance of a more full-figured body**.

One of the solutions that can guarantee a nice outcome, creating a proportional figure and adding length to your legs while balancing the volume of the upper body, is **choosing sweaters that come just under the buttocks** and pairing them with **skinny pants and heels** (as in the picture on the right). This combination, as we have previously seen, hides the actual length of the leg with a slender overall effect.

It's **better to avoid the combination with wide pants**, as you see on the left, because they make the legs larger and shorter (besides, here there is an additional widening effect due to the "bulky" waistline of the trousers, adding extra volume around the waist), while in the image on the right, the silhouette looks longer. Also, **be careful in picking out colors**: it's important that there is **no chromatic contrast between boot and trousers,** because, as you see in the picture in the middle, a stark contrast between pants and ankle boots makes the legs look shorter (with a knee-high boot, it's different, as we will encounter later).

68. How to choose knee-high boots

Knee boots, in addition to being comfortable and warm, lend themselves to a lot of combinations. However, **for those who would like to look taller or thinner, they require some basic cautions**.

One of the most important things to consider is **the length of the boot itself**: for those who do not have long legs, it's frequent that the boot arrives exactly at the knee (instead of ending a few inches below), which, in addition to being totally uncomfortable, also winds up **shortening the figure**, as you can see in the picture on the left. Legs look shorter (despite the high heel), and besides they also look knock-kneed—even if they aren't—because of the optical effect of the boot that is too wide on the exterior part of the leg.

The answer? **Look for boots that do not have an excessive length** (this may require some time, but it can also be a useful way to pick out quality items). Or otherwise **you can have the boot shortened by a good shoemaker**.

69. Never wear knee boots under the pants

Still on the subject of knee boots, remember that, regardless of your weight and height, pairing **knee boots with skinny pants** usually is **not the most flattering solution for those who would like to hide some extra pounds around hips or thighs**. This is particularly true if the upper part of the leg is comparatively shorter than the lower one. **Instead, this option can be helpful for those that have the lower part of the leg proportionally shorter** than the upper one (like I do) because it helps to hide the disproportion, as you see in the picture on the right. For those who have bulky thighs, it's better to choose the combination of boot-cut pants and ankle boots, as in tip 45. **If you are thinking of wearing the pants *over* the boot**, there is only one answer: **do not do it**! Under the trousers, you can wear only ankle boots. **Knee boots cannot be worn under the pants**; they just add extra inches to your calf, as you can see on the left: the trousers remain wrapped around the boots, with the effect of making the leg look bulky and short, even with a high heel.

70. Pair a long sweater with knee boots

A very effective way to wear **wide, long sweaters** is to **match them with skinny pants and pair them with knee boots** with at least a medium heel (two inches can be enough). This type of solution, although not the most flattering one, still has a pleasant outcome thanks to the fact that **the actual length of the legs remains hidden**. With this outfit, **the leg itself goes almost completely unnoticed**, unlike what happens if you match the same outfit with ankle boots or with sneakers (or even pumps). As you can see from the comparison between the pictures below, **on the left, the legs look short and bulky** because the sweater that reaches mid-thigh visually shortens the legs (despite the use of monochrome). Conversely, **on the right, the overall effect**, though not particularly slim because of the sweater that is a bit too long, **makes the figure harmonious enough** because it does not highlight the (little) length of the leg.

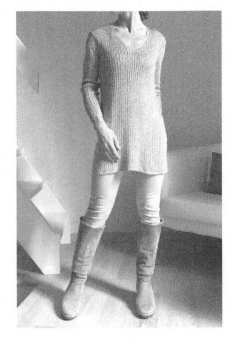

71. Wear long, open cardigans over a contrasting outfit

Another way to wear wide, long knitwear is to pick out **long cardigans, to be worn over a monochrome outfit** (preferably dark) in a color that contrasts with the hue of the cardigan.

This outfit visually creates a slim silhouette that stretches out the figure while adding a few inches to the legs.

However, some considerations are needed: first, to balance out the width and volume of the cardigan, **everything else should be as close-fitting** as possible, as in the picture on the right (if the sweater is too large, as in the picture on the left, the volume becomes excessive).

And for the same reason, it is better to **choose footwear with a bit of heel** in order to reduce the potentially shortening effect of the long sweater. And in all cases, it is best to **avoid cardigans that reach to the knees and beyond**, because they would shorten the figure excessively.

72. How to pair footwear with skirts

As we have already seen previously, and as we will encounter shortly, for those who would like to visually cut off a few extra pounds or wish to appear taller, the most suitable skirts are **A-line skirts, as well as those that have a flared silhouette**. As for pairing them with footwear, in winter, if you want to look slimmer or taller, the ideal solution is choosing **knee boots**, which, when matched **with a skirt, are also suitable for those who would like to reduce the circumference of the hips or thighs**. Among other things, as knee boots camouflage a good part of the leg, they can be worn with different skirt patterns. The heel can be either high or low, though of course high heels (or at least medium ones) are more suitable for those who would like to add a few inches to the legs. Besides, also consider that **high-heeled boots can be far more comfortable than a pump** that has the same heel height, because heels can be slightly thicker (while thick heels are not the most slimming choice with pumps). Generally speaking, it is better to **avoid ankle boots that, when paired with skirts, visually divide the leg** (which does not happen with knee-boots, for the simple reason that they come where the leg already "breaks"). Two exceptions: **lace-up ankle-boots** that match with the tone of stockings, because they **do not have the visual effect of cutting the legs**; and boots with high, thin heels combined with long, flared skirts, provided that the skirt is long enough to hide the upper part of the ankle boot. As for pairing skirts with pumps, in the winter it is a not always an easy choice **because choosing the right stocking can be quite hard**. On this subject, remember that **if you have bulky calves**, it's better to **avoid a medium thickness** (the classic twenty denier tights) because they would become darker on the ankle, where the fabric is less stretched, and almost transparent on the calf, **highlighting exactly what you want to hide**. Better to wear dark, thicker tights (dark cotton pantyhose have a lovely outcome) or, conversely, very thin ones (seven to eight denier, no more). Also, be careful with fancy stockings, which can highlight any imperfections.

73. Skirts: Go monochrome

In Part 1 of the book, we saw that in the summertime, a dress can be preferable to a skirt, mainly because a summer dress can have a slimming effect. **In winter**, though, **skirts may be the easiest option**. Why? Because the slimming effect of the summer dress is due to the fact that it is sleeveless, thanks to the uninterrupted vertical line that visually lengthens the silhouette. **If a dress is not sleeveless, conversely, the vertical thin line does not exist whatsoever**, and the overall effect can widen your figure. For this reason, in winter, wearing a skirt can be highly preferable than wearing a dress. If you want to achieve the most flattering results, **it is better to match a skirt with a sweater that is in tone** with the skirt, **quite close-fitting**, and preferably **turtleneck** (to elongate the silhouette). As you can see in the pictures below, matching contrasting colors shortens the body, while coordinating tones (as in the picture on the right) makes the silhouette slender. Warning: "similar colors" does not mean identical, but colors that have a similar brightness.

74. How to choose the pattern of a skirt

It's well-known that **flared lines are the most suitable ones to make the legs look longer and slender** because, for an optical effect, they reduce the circumference of the legs, making them look slimmer and adding a few inches to their length. This rule applies even in the winter months, though it is less mandatory, thanks to the dark stockings that eliminate the gap between leg and footwear, allowing you to play with many different patterns. Also, you should remember that, **in winter, too-wide skirts may have an unexpected drawback**, because the great amount of heavy fabric can easily add a few pounds to your hips. For this reason, it's better to choose with caution the pattern of this garment. **The most flattering one is a slightly flared line** like the one you see on the right, which has a slimming effect thanks to its linear pattern, which does not have too much fabric nor too many stitches. Conversely, **a straight skirt** (on the left) **increases the waist and hip circumference** while at the same time making the legs look bigger.

75. Shorten straight skirts

Still on the subject of skirts, **if you want to wear a straight one, then it's better if it's reasonably short**. As you see below, when the skirt comes to the knee (on the left), it makes the leg look shorter while widening the whole figure. Conversely, when shortening the same skirt, adjusting the hem to mid-thigh (on the right), it helps to hide the hips, and the overall effect is a slimmer figure. Another hint: as encountered in tip 73, the ideal sweater to match to a skirt should also be preferably close-fitting, even better if it's turtleneck. Why? Because **the skirt has a widening effect on the silhouette, and a slim pullover can help balance this out**. For the same reason, it's better not to pair a skirt with wide knitwear (which looks so lovely with skinny pants) unless you want to look all bundled-up. To maximize the slimming effect, it is also better to wear a **turtleneck** that always **enhances your breasts while lengthening the silhouette** (and if you are small-busted, wear a padded bra!) and guarantees a flattering outcome on the whole figure.

76. Flattering details: Lengths and widths

In winter, the amount of clothing we wear requires taking some care to **balance lengths and widths**, obtaining a proportionate and a pleasantly harmonious figure.

One of the first things to consider—which is especially true if you frequently wear a blazer or if you layer clothing that has heavy fabric—is that **your coat should be large enough to allow you to move your arms comfortably**. Otherwise, all you get is **a kind of a "sausage effect" that is totally awkward** for any type of physical build.

When in doubt, then, choose a coat that is one size larger than your usual one, giving preference to items with **belts that allow you to shape the excessive volume of your clothes**. A belt, as we have seen in many points, may be very useful indeed to make your figure slimmer, especially for those who are not tall. As every short-statured girl knows too well, **a shapeless outfit matched with legs that are not so long always has an enlarging effect**, adding extra pounds even where you don't have any. For this reason, it is always better to **highlight the waistline, possibly wearing the belt slightly higher** than your actual waistline so as to lengthen the legs.

For the same reason, **long coats are generally unsuitable for those who are quite short**. If you really like them, always pair them with the tallest heels you can wear, hidden under boot-cut pants.

Always, for those who love layering, **pay attention to long cardigans**: their hems must *never* extend beyond the coat! If you realize it after you are already out of the house, try to make a knot with the cardigan to shorten it (and remember to loosen the knot when removing your coat!).

77. Use necklaces strategically

Accessories, we have seen, can be crucial in balancing the figure, as they may **highlight your strong points while hiding many imperfections**. In winter an effective way to bring attention away from what you want to be hidden is **playing around with jewelry, especially necklaces**. First of all, let's make it clear that when talking about "jewelry," we also mean items not necessarily expensive (like the one in the picture on the right). Secondly, remember that in many cases, the mere act of **adding something in a bright material to a dark and monochromatic outfit can be a really flattering solution**, which is also classy and chic. Even if many women assume that **"all-black"** means "slimming," that's not always the case. Conversely, a similar outfit **can also be not flattering at all**, as you can see on the left. **Just by adding a long, bright necklace**, though, you can **enhance your figure**, creating a point that catalyzes attention, distracting it from your hips, and also—thanks to its vertical line—creating a slenderizing effect on the entire figure.

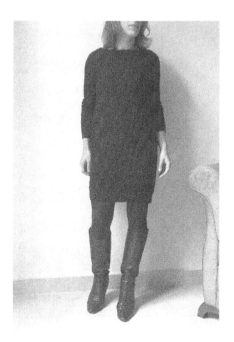 

78. Wear short, knit dresses

As seen in point 73, **in winter a dress can be an unflattering choice** because, as explained, a dress can be extra-slimming when sleeveless, while the sleeves add volume to the figure—especially for those who are quite short-statured. Besides, **heavy fabric and lining can give the impression of a more full-figured body**, and for this reason, it's better to avoid it if you are not very tall. **An exception**, however, is the **knit dress**, as long as it is **quite short** (always above the knee, better if mid-thigh; if you pair it with heavy tights, it can be worn at all ages) and **paired with high boots**. This garment does not have seams or linings that widen the body; it **gently follows the silhouette and softly smoothes bulges**. However, as mentioned, it should be quite short and preferably turtleneck (as in the picture on the right), and preferably slightly formfitting, thanks to a belt. A longer length (on the left) instead enlarges the body. The ideal pairing is to wear it with knee boots; **pairing it with ankle boots it is only suitable for those who are very tall**.

79. Unbutton your shirt—Part 2

As encountered in points 13 and 55, both for summer months and for spring and autumn, **garments buttoned to the neck can enlarge the figure** if you are not very tall or slim (*note: this does not mean turtleneck knitwear, but items that actually have buttons*). You can make use of this hint also in winter—making the most of your strong points and taking advantage of your curves rather than hiding them—even when wearing a shirt under V-neck knitwear.

As you can see in the pictures below, **the buttoned shirt** *(left)* **makes the figure look more full-bodied**, whereas by just **unbuttoning a few buttons** like on the right (without necessarily showing your entire cleavage), you can get a slimmer effect.

Besides being **pleasantly mischievous**, this lovely outcome positively affects your entire shape, because the neckline visually reduces the height of your bust while making your legs look comparatively longer. Moreover, a neckline always brightens your face, which in winter can be a very good thing, indeed.

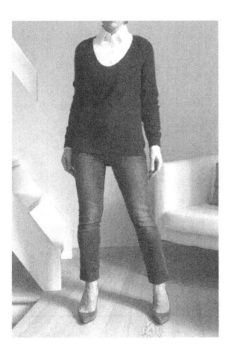 

80. How to pair ankle sneakers

In the winter months, sneakers can become more challenging to wear, not so much for temperature reasons (sneaker addicts wear them even at twenty degrees below zero), but mainly because **the most common winter pattern usually reaches the ankle**, which frequently has the disadvantage of **cutting the figure shorter**.

The simplest choice to get the best results is usually to match this type of footwear with **straight pants in the same tone as that of the sweater** (or of the jacket). Coordinating tones, as we have often pointed out, is an easy way **to create a long, continuous line** (as in the image on the right) that **balances out the widening effect of the ankle shoe** (while on the left, the widening effect of the sneakers is emphasized).

Another option is to wear boot-cut pants, which, thanks to their flared line, always slenderize the silhouette, allowing greater freedom in the choice of footwear.

81. Make careful use of wedges

Wedge sneakers undoubtedly are a very trendy item, especially among the younger generation, because they **combine the comfort of sneakers with some extra inche**s that the wedge adds to the legs.

However, wearing wedges requires particular attention, because it's essential to **entirely camouflage the disproportion between the wedges and the calf**. As you can see below, **if you match the wedge sneaker with skinny pants** (on the left) or leave them in plain sight, **the outcome is, beyond any doubt, really terrible**. The shoe is longer than the calf, the leg looks incredibly short, and let's not even begin to think about what could happen when wearing a coat that comes to the knee. In the picture on the right, instead, **the same sneaker is matched with boot-cut trousers**, which completely hide the wedge, thus **eliminating any disproportion**; the effect, as you can see, is absolutely lovely and very slimming!

 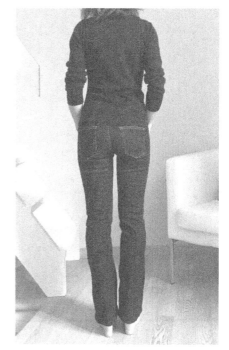

82. Wear knee boots with contrasting hues—1

Knee boots, as we've seen, can have the advantage of **making the length of the leg less noticeable**, visually lengthening the figure. This flattering effect is higher with high heels but still remains with lower heels. Furthermore, there are also boots with a small inner wedge that can guarantee excellent results as well. You can, therefore, **take advantage of this item when playing with contrasts**, which are a lovely and more interesting alternative to the ordinary—and indeed quite boring—all-black outfit. Anyway, be aware that **to obtain a slimming effect, it's mandatory to wear only boots that come to the knee** (as you see on the right). With ankle boots (on the left), conversely, the outcome is precisely the opposite. In fact, **ankle boots, coming halfway up the calf, visually break the leg** (this is more evident when they are paired with coats that come to the knee), while **knee boots create a long, vertical line** that adds length to the legs, elongating the whole figure.

83. Wear knee boots with contrasting hues—2

Continuing on the subject of knee boots and contrasting colors, we will now see how, when wearing garments that create a **stark contrast between the upper and lower body**, the shortening effect of the ankle boots is not mitigated even by matching the boot to a similar color of pants (in this case, black). In fact, as you can see on the left, **pairing a light-colored coat with dark ankle boots makes the figure look shorter**, because the shortening effect of the ankle boots is still there, even if it has the same color of the pants (and **also in the presence of a very high heel**). Conversely, knee boots (on the right) elongate the line of the legs. **If you want to play around with contrasts, then it is crucial to wear knee boots**, or alternatively wear boot-cut pants (as in tip 45). If you want to keep ankle boots in plain sight, then choose a monochrome outfit (trousers, knit, coat, everything; see point 67). If the whole outfit seems boring, you can always liven it up with a bright-colored bag (see point 51).

84. Use turtlenecks to play with colors

Another way to take advantage of flattering colors and shapes while playing around with contrasts is **layering a boat-neck, light-colored pullover to a darker ensemble of skinny pants and turtleneck, formfitting sweater**—preferably wearing shoes of the same color as the sweater (picture on the right).

This outfit, which is also very suitable for those who are fond of vintage fashion because it takes you back to the '60s or something, **works to lengthen the silhouette despite being slightly overdressed** because the continuity of colors between the turtleneck and the pants **creates a long, vertical line, regardless of the contrasting pullover**. Conversely, if you remove the dark turtleneck (on the left), the effect is not flattering at all. Hint: **this can work wonderfully also with light-colored ponchos**. Another tip: as mentioned at the beginning of the book, in the pictures I mainly make use of neutral colors, but this is just to facilitate understanding. Of course, you can use the colors that you like the most and that are the most suitable for you.

85. Wear long, flared, contrasting blazers

The **blazer** is a garment that is not always easy for women who wish to create the impression of a longer, leaner body, because if not appropriately paired, it **can potentially enlarge and shorten the figure** (as seen in the picture on the left) with counterproductive effects for those who want to look thinner. In winter one of the ways to wear a blazer flawlessly is to **choose flared lines that cover the hips**, so you can hide a few extra pounds while taking advantage of the flared line that slims your waistline, **creating the visual effect of an hourglass figure** (it looks like it's the blazer that is widening, not your hips).

Another hint, similar to what we saw for overcoats and coats (points 41 and 61), is to **pair contrasting colors,** because you can **visually create a vertical line that works double time to lengthen your silhouette**. You can also combine this outfit with contrasting boots like those in the pictures below if you like, but the slimming effect is obviously greater with boots that have the same color as the pants.

86. Trousers: Avoid fancy fabrics

Fancy fabrics trousers are usually not very easy to wear for those who would like to look taller and slimmer because they inevitably **focus the attention on the legs**, so it's better to wear them with caution. **In winter, it would be better to completely avoid this garment**, because, as we have seen, when wearing coats that come to the knee, there is just a small part of the leg that remains in plain sight, so it's better to style it with care (which means avoid widening items like fancy fabrics). As you can see in the photo on the left, even choosing a fabric with a quite toned-down print—even with neutral colors like black and white—the effect is not slimming at all (even with heels). Wearing a short coat could seem like a nice alternative, though this option still does not actually produce a satisfactory outcome. It is better to **stay on the safe side and wear solid-colored pants**, taking advantage of **handbags and accessories if you want to brighten your look** (see tips 51 and 54).

87. Accessories: Match warm and cool hues

Another element that can flatter your silhouette in multiple ways is **pairing complementary hues**. Carefully choosing the colors of the outfit as well as those of the accessories can help **brighten your appearance**, adding the visual effect of **a thinner and harmonious figure**.

The best pairings are complementary tones, as well as matching warm and cool colors. This way you can **balance the whole figure while obtaining a lovely silhouette** thanks to a wise combination of hues and proportions. Hint: the results are better if you can apply this tip to **accessories that remain in sight even when wearing the coat,** such as scarves, handbags, and shoes, and playing around with their shades to balance the ensemble. In the left image, for example, the bright bag helps to brighten a dark outfit (and the shoes, even if dark, have a hue similar to that of the bag). The scarf knotted to the bag can also be wrapped around the neck. On the right, the warm brown tones match with the blue tones of the outfit.

88. Flattering contrasts: Light-colored outfits

The combination of **contrasting colors**, as we've seen in many tips, usually gives the best results by overlaying a light-colored garment (a shirt, a coat, a jacket) on a dark-colored outfit, because this ensemble creates a long, thin silhouette, which is emphasized by the dark color. In the winter, though, you can apply this hint even by inverting the colors, that means **using a more intense color overlaid with a fairly light-colored outfit**. Why? Because with winter clothing, usually, the leg is completely covered. The multiple gaps between shoe/leg/trousers disappear, and instead, you have a long, **uninterrupted vertical line that is slender, albeit clear**.

As you can see in the pictures below, the coat paired with contrasting trousers (on the left) has a widening effect, while worn open on a light-colored outfit (on the right), it **slims and stretches out the figure**. Hint: you can obtain the same result by merely **wearing a light-colored scarf over the dark coat, so as to visually extend the line of the legs**.

89. Pair a light-colored outfit with knee boots

Light-colored garments are habitually worn more frequently in spring or summer, but, if you like these shades, **you can use them even in the winter**, as we said above.

The only recommendation is to **avoid full white, giving preference to softer shades** that can be beige tones if you like warm hues or light-gray tones for those who prefer cool shades. **If you want to reduce the possibly widening effect** that can come when wearing light-colored garments, **you can coordinate tones**, choosing outfits entirely made up of light colors. Usually, it's better to **use lighter tones for your upper body** while the hues gradually become slightly darker for your lower body, as in the pictures below.

Furthermore, **it is highly preferable to pair this outfit with knee boots**. In fact, knee boots have the effect of camouflaging the actual leg length (picture on the right), while the shoes highlight the leg, emphasizing the widening effect of the light-colored outfit (picture on the left).

90. Carry light-colored handbags

Still on the subject of accessories, and in particular on the subject of handbags, **in winter the most common choice is usually to carry dark-colored bags**. However, even if some may assume that dark tonalities are the easiest option—lending themselves to pairings with many different outfits—this is not always the case. Conversely, as we also encountered in tip 51, **when pairing a dark-colored handbag to a similarly dark-colored outfit**, you can get the unpleasant outcome of **widening the whole figure, adding volume and extra pounds just where you don't need to** (as on the left). The alternative? **Always choose a handbag in a contrasting color with the rest of the outfit** (among other things, as it draws attention to itself, any imperfection remains unnoticed). If you keep it in neutral tones like light gray (on the right), you will still have a passe-partout color. One more hint: **the "contrasting-color approach" also work for gloves**; light-colored gloves paired with a dark coat shorten your arms while making your legs look comparatively longer.

PART 4

Eleven Hints
that are
Always
Effective

Conclusion

When I was in first grade in elementary school, occasionally the "big" girls from the fifth grade came to my class.

Among these, there were two particularly tall ones who, sitting on our small chairs, reached the floor with their knees.

I remember that every single time, I used to say to myself, "How many years will I have to wait for *my* knees to reach the floor?"

Today, with my height of five foot two, I'm still waiting.

Now, another flashback: I was twelve, and while approaching the semi-open door of the kitchen, I heard my parents say about me, "What should we do? Neither of us is fat."

After that, for many years, it was an uninterrupted succession of diets and shapeless clothing to conceal my entirely imaginary extra pounds (I was not fat, indeed, just a bit chubby, as many teenagers are). Then, in my twenties, I turned to the exact opposite approach: plunging necklines and extra-short skirts to draw attention to something other than my low height.

For years I considered myself irremediably overweight, large, and stocky because of my not exactly thin—and also quite short—legs, and because of my stature (which perhaps is not that incredibly short, but is undeniably below average).

I actually became slimmer, but I always had the feeling of carrying around a lot of extra pounds.

Then, little by little, I realized that the best way to accomplish my goals was simply shaping my silhouette and taking advantage of my strong points, thanks to a few easy "optical tricks" that could give the illusion of a taller-appearing figure.

I learned how to make the most of my physique, which, even if quite short-statured, could really become lovely, making me feel attractive and beautiful beyond any doubt.

You've read, in the previous chapters, the main rules to follow if you want to enhance your appearance with the help of flattering clothes and combinations that can make you longer and leaner.

In the next pages, you will find a summary of those that I think are the most important points, those from which to start—put them into practice!

Maybe at first it will not be easy, and it will take a while to take full advantage of them.

But in no time—trust my words—you will able to see the results, and you won't believe your eyes!

91. Avoid wide, high-hemmed pants

As we've seen in many passages, if you want a taller-appearing figure, visually cutting off a few pounds, the best choice for **trousers** is choosing styles that are **quite close-fitting without being too tight** (straight models that come to the ankle, as on the right) **or flared ones paired with heels** (as long as the heel remains hidden under the pants).

Conversely, if you choose **high-hemmed pants with a wide leg**, you get the result of **shortening your figure while enlarging your legs**—and indeed, your whole body. Wide trousers, if not properly balanced out by very high heels, **just take off inches in length while adding inches to the circumference**, as you can see on the left. That being said, it's equally true that wide (or baggy), high-hemmed pants are now back into style. Well, if you're not tall, *forget them!* **Wide trousers can have a slimming effect only on those who are very tall** because they can balance out the width with the length of the legs. But if you are not exactly tall, they can have horrible effects!

92. Never wear too many loose-fitting clothes

This rule is undoubtedly one of the most known ones. Though, it is useful to point it out once more to fully understand—with the help of the images—that a careful choice can completely change your appearance. This is because, as we already pointed out, **people perceive your clothing much more, indeed, than your actual figure**, so you'd better take advantage of it. When saying "never wear too many loose-fitting clothes" we mean the importance of (1) **drawing attention to the thinner parts of your figure** (such as ankles or waist, if you're lucky enough to have a slim waistline), or to the most flattering ones (as a lovely cleavage can be) and (2) choosing **shaping fits and fabrics that highlight your curves instead of covering them**. When wearing only large, wide garments, the outcome is not flattering at all, as you can see in the photo on the left. Conversely, **matching a wide item to a more close-fitting one** (for example, a soft pullover paired with skinny pants), you can get a slimmer effect, as you can see in the picture on the right.

93. Avoid "all-tight" ensembles

The previous rule also applies to the opposite. Choosing **shaping garments that enhance your strong points** and highlight your curves instead of covering them **does not mean wearing clothing three sizes too small** but rather finding the **items that are just right for you**. Extra-tight garments draw attention to any imperfection you may have and make you look less slender. Also, for those who are quite short-statured, it may be even more counterproductive to wear only formfitting garments because they make the legs look shorter, as you can see in the image below on the left. Better to **play around with proportions and contrasts**, which allow you to modify the perception of the silhouette while flattering the whole body, which can be achieved by choosing **close-fitting, but not too tight, garments** (as on the right). In fact, if your clothes are too revealing, you cannot apply tricks of any kind. Conversely, carefully playing with fits and colors, besides making you seem slimmer, **gives you a more interesting, elegant, and intriguing look**.

94. Skirts: Avoid "short and tight"

As we have explained in many passages of the book, when picking out **skirts and dresses,** it is usually better to **avoid fits that are excessively tight**.

This rule is especially true for miniskirts or for dresses that end above the knee (as you can see in the picture on the left); in fact, wearing **a short, form-fitting skirt** winds up **making the legs look bulkier and even shorter**.

For miniskirts and mini-dresses, therefore, give preference to **A-lines or flared models,** that, for an optical effect, always help to **make the legs look slimmer,** as seen in points 7, 17, 29, and 74. **The same is valid also for skirts or dresses that come to the middle of the calf.** Even in this case, avoid formfitting garments and give preference to lines that are wider in the lower part. **If you want to wear tight skirts** or dresses, **the ideal length is knee-length** (as in the picture on the right), preferably paired with heels.

So the rule is: tight skirt (or dress) = knee length + heels.

95. Heels: Some tips

Heels, as we have seen in many tips, should always be chosen and matched with the appropriate arrangements because in some cases, **instead of enhancing the figure, they can even—oddly enough—wind up shortening it**.

So let's have a quick look at the main rules to remember:

(1) **Never wear heels with capri pants**. As you can see in the photo on the left, for an optical effect, if you do not have a skinny leg (and calf), they shorten your leg, especially from behind; the ideal pairing is with ballet flats (photo in the center).

(2) **No platforms, please**! Especially with winter shoes, and even more so if they are dark. **Instead of adding some inches in height, they add them in width** and are therefore only suitable for those who are tall and slender (and not all of them, either).

(3) When wearing **knee pants,** it's usually better to **pair them with heels, unless you have very thin legs**. In summer, you can also pick out sandals with wedges (as on the right), but keep it quite toned-down, or you will fall under heading 2.

 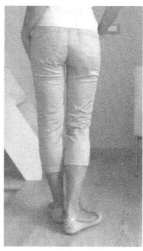 

96. Wear low necklines

One of the best tricks that always works to add a few inches to the legs is to **take advantage of low necklines**. In fact, a neckline works double time to make your figure thinner and leaner, because, for an optical reason, it lengthens the legs. This is because **showing some skin around your neck** reduces your bust, while **the legs look comparatively longer, and the whole figure is flattered**. To make the most of this hint and get a very French chic look, you can **match the color of the shirt to that of the shoes**, as in the pictures below. Remember, though, that in addition to low necklines *(which do not necessarily need to be very deep)*, if you want a proportionate figure while drawing attention to the slimmest points of your body, **it's better if your ankles also remain in plain sight.** As we also encountered in points 21, 55, and 79, and as in the image on the right, this is mainly true when wearing sneakers. If the silhouette of the paints is straight, this flatters the leg, making it look more tapered, while on the left, the legs seem shorter and the figure less harmonious.

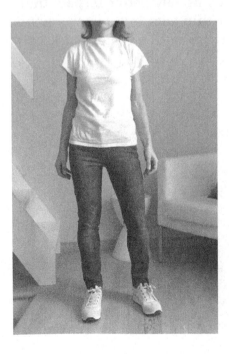 

97. ...and take advantage of turtlenecks

As an alternative to low necklines, you can also get a slimming effect with **turtleneck sweaters**, as long as they are quite close-fitting, as in the image on the right. This hint works best when **coordinating dark tones**.

In fact, if you wear a turtleneck sweater in a similar shade to that of the pants, this creates **an uninterrupted, vertical line that flatters your figure** in multiple ways. **A dark turtleneck emphasizes one of the thinner parts of your body (the neck), adding length to it** and working on elongating the whole silhouette. Conversely, when the sweater has no turtleneck, and it has not a low neckline (on the left), it draws attention to a short neck, making the entire body look shorter. For this reason, tight crew neck sweaters are to be used with care if you want like to look slimmer or taller. As for the colors, remember that turtleneck garments need more attention because they are close to your face (as there is no "visual filter" provided by the neckline), so **choose only among colors that work best for your skin tone**.

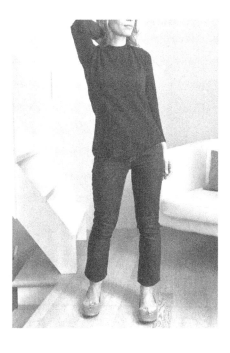 

98. Make the most of contrasts

Playing around with contrasts, as mentioned in many points of this book, is usually **highly preferable to a dull, all-dark outfit**. *(This is not the case, though, when talking about all-white outfits, which in summertime can make the figure slimmer).* Just as the "all-wide" and the "all-tight" approaches are to be avoided—as a more balanced choice allows you to get a more balanced figure—when it comes to colors, the best results come by **playing around with contrasting tonalities**, which can also allow you to achieve a much more elegant and chic look. As you can see below, **the only choice to avoid is a *total* contrast of colors between bust and legs** (and particularly if the item that you choose for your upper body is quite long, because it adds extra inches to your bust while shortening the legs). As opposed to what you would think, **you can get a lovely outcome using contrasts "vertically"** to reduce the width of the silhouette, while lengthening the legs and slimming the whole body. This can be achieved **maintaining a chromatic continuity between above and below**.

Continuity can be given by trousers and tops (with contrasting blazer), as in the center, or trousers and blazer (with contrasting tops) as on the right. The result is always slimming and in all cases very chic.

99. Flattering accessories:
Contrasting shoes and handbags

As pointed out in tip 98, if you want to give the impression of a thinner figure, you can take advantage of **accessories whose colors contrast with the outfit** (handbags, footwear, scarves, belts, or jewelry). This solution, can **flatter your figure in multiple ways** while enhancing your silhouette. This hint works for two main reasons: **Accessories whose color is different** from that of the outfit **do not add volume to the body** (as on the left). (2) If **the accessories draw attention to themselves, any imperfection becomes less noticeable**. But beware: the outfit below must be monochromatic (better if darker). And besides, when coordinating items, **the hues do not necessarily have to be identical**. If a tone is quite bright, it is better to pair it with softer tones: natural leather, for example, lends itself to infinite combinations with mustard, orange, red, or yellow. And, needless to say, the color combinations must be of good taste; otherwise, they will draw attention, but maybe not the kind you want.

100. Wear white sneakers

Sneakers are indeed one of the favorite items of many women. However, **they are not the most suitable choice for those who would like to look taller or think they have a few extra pounds**, because the absence of any heel compounds the fact that they cover the foot almost entirely, so there's no way to take advantage of the lengthening effect that ballet flats can have when properly paired. That being said, you can still wear them with some satisfaction if you just **shorten the hem of the trousers so that the ankle is visible** (as in the picture on the right). As we have seen on several occasions, leaving the slimmest part of the leg in plain sight helps to make the whole figure look slimmer (whereas hiding the ankle, as on the left, makes the figure look shorter). And besides, don't forget **that the result is better with light-colored sneakers** (not just white). Instead, **darker colors** (as in the picture on the left) are to be avoided because **for an optical effect, they give the impression of a thicker leg** (even if they have a wedge, as is the case below!).

101. Fabrics: Look for quality

Last but not least, another very important hint: if your goal is to enhance your silhouette, the best way to accomplish your target is to **choose quality fabrics**. Why? Aside from the fact that **lovely materials help you achieve a very chic, classy, and elegant look** and a unique allure, they also enhance your whole body, **helping your silhouette look more toned**.

Low-quality materials, conversely, frequently show unpleasant folds and pleats that wind up **amplifying every imperfection** and every single extra pound. If not properly supportive and "shaping," they easily **highlight any fault in your figure—even where the fault, in fact, doesn't exist** (as in tips 10 and 22).

The most suitable choice is, therefore, to choose **lightly shaping fabrics** (not stiff, though, or ballooning) or very soft fabrics **that follow the shape of your body while hiding what you want to keep hidden**. It's always better to give preference to natural materials such as cotton, linen, and silk. Also pick out those that have a slight stretch, which allows you to have a kind of "sheath" effect; properly chosen fabrics can **smooth bulges while visually cutting off inches where you would like to**.

The bad news (not so new) is that **many of these fabrics are not cheap at all**. The good news, though, is that luckily enough, there are also items that you can buy even at totally reasonable prices. So if you want to get the best results, you just have to be wise: spend only for what has to be good quality (knitwear, shoes, handbags, some classic trousers, and shirts), and keep a low budget for items that can be found at reasonable prices (jeans, some tops, underwear, belts, scarves).

One more hint: **when you buy good-quality** items—which will last for years—it is important to **avoid "trendy" styles** (which you will not want to wear anymore within one year) and choose the classic colors and fits that will also assure you **a unique elegance and a style (*your* style!) that is really timeless**.

About the Author

Chiara Giuliani, an architect with a passion for style and fashion, lives in Florence, Italy. After some academic and professional publications, in 2012 she published her first book, La Casa di Charme, *a manual for making your home your own unique place, with hints to make spaces look visually bigger and more proportionate. In 2016, she published her second book,* La Donna di Charme *(translated to English under the title* How to Become a Woman of *Charme), a manual of personal style to provide women of all ages and types with the tools to build their self-confidence by enhancing their strong points, and to help them feel more beautiful and attractive. In 2017, in collaboration with her cousin Benedetta Belloni who has been working for years in the field of custom-made luxury garments, she founded the website* www.ladonnadicharme.it. *This book, which develops and deepens some posts published on the website, provides useful suggestions that help flatter the figure and make the most of your strategic points, visually stretching out the silhouette and allowing those who would like to look slimmer or taller to get a slender figure, giving all women an immediate tool for improving their image, thus increasing their self-esteem.*

Her motto comes from a famous quote:

**Beauty begins
the moment you decide
to be yourself.**
—Coco Chanel

www.ladonnadicharme.it

**Follow us on Instagram
@ladonnadicharme**

Made in the USA
Monee, IL
12 February 2020